$18.95

THE
CREEKS

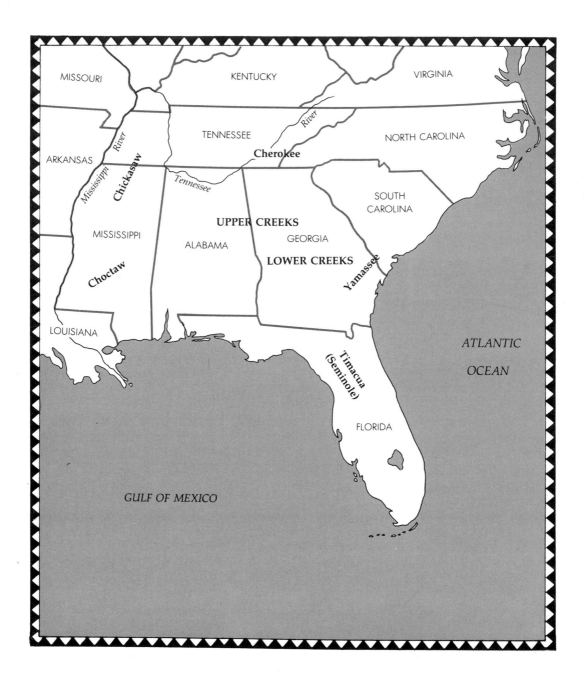

MISSOURI

KENTUCKY

VIRGINIA

TENNESSEE

River

NORTH CAROLINA

ARKANSAS

Cherokee

Mississippi River

Chickasaw

Tennessee

SOUTH
CAROLINA

UPPER CREEKS

MISSISSIPPI

ALABAMA

GEORGIA

LOWER CREEKS

Choctaw

Yamassee

LOUISIANA

ATLANTIC

OCEAN

**Timacua
(Seminole)**

FLORIDA

GULF OF MEXICO

THE
CREEKS

Michael D. Green
Dartmouth College

Frank W. Porter III
General Editor

CHELSEA HOUSE PUBLISHERS
New York   Philadelphia

On the cover   A velvet hat decorated with beaded floral geometric patterns. The cap was made in the 1820s by a Creek Indian for U.S. Army general Edmund P. Gaines, who conducted a fact-finding mission among the Creeks.

Chelsea House Publishers
Editor-in-Chief   Nancy Toff
Executive Editor   Remmel T. Nunn
Managing Editor   Karyn Gullen Browne
Copy Chief   Juliann Barbato
Picture Editor   Adrian G. Allen
Art Director   Maria Epes
Manufacturing Manager   Gerald Levine

Indians of North America
Senior Editor   Liz Sonneborn

Staff for **THE CREEKS**
Assistant Editor   Claire Wilson
Deputy Copy Chief   Mark Rifkin
Copy Editor   Richard Klin
Editorial Assistant   Nicole Claro
Assistant Art Director   Loraine Machlin
Designer   Donna Sinisgalli
Assistant Designer   James Baker
Picture Researcher   Diana Gongora
Production Manager   Joseph Romano
Production Coordinator   Marie Claire Cebrián

5   7   9   8   6   4

Library of Congress Cataloging-in-Publication Data

Green, Michael D.
The Creek/Michael D. Green.
p.   cm.—(Indians of North America)
Includes bibliographical references.
Summary: Examines the culture, history, and changing fortunes of the Creek Indians.
ISBN 1-55546-703-7
    0-7910-0378-7 (pbk.)
1. Creek Indians.   [1. Creek Indians.   2. Indians of North America.]   I. Title.   II. Series: Indians of North America (Chelsea House Publishers)   89-37071
E99.C9G738   1990   CIP
973'.04973—dc20   AC

CONTENTS

INDIANS OF NORTH AMERICA

CHELSEA HOUSE PUBLISHERS

INDIANS OF NORTH AMERICA: CONFLICT AND SURVIVAL

Frank W. Porter III

The Indians survived our open intention of wiping them out, and since the tide turned they have even weathered our good intentions toward them, which can be much more deadly.

John Steinbeck
America and Americans

When Europeans first reached the North American continent, they found hundreds of tribes occupying a vast and rich country. The newcomers quickly recognized the wealth of natural resources. They were not, however, so quick or willing to recognize the spiritual, cultural, and intellectual riches of the people they called Indians.

The Indians of North America examines the problems that develop when people with different cultures come together. For American Indians, the consequences of their interaction with non-Indian people have been both productive and tragic. The Europeans believed they had "discovered" a "New World," but their religious bigotry, cultural bias, and materialistic world view kept them from appreciating and understanding the people who lived in it. All too often they attempted to change the way of life of the indigenous people. The Spanish conquistadores wanted the Indians as a source of labor. The Christian missionaries, many of whom were English, viewed them as potential converts. French traders and trappers used the Indians as a means to obtain pelts. As Francis Parkman, the 19th-century historian, stated, "Spanish civilization crushed the Indian; English civilization scorned and neglected him; French civilization embraced and cherished him."

Nearly 500 years later, many people think of American Indians as curious vestiges of a distant past, waging a futile war to survive in a Space Age society. Even today, our understanding of the history and culture of American Indians is too often derived from unsympathetic, culturally biased, and inaccurate reports. The American Indian, described and portrayed in thousands of movies, television programs, books, articles, and government studies, has either been raised to the status of the "noble savage" or disparaged as the "wild Indian" who resisted the westward expansion of the American frontier.

Where in this popular view are the real Indians, the human beings and communities whose ancestors can be traced back to ice-age hunters? Where are the creative and indomitable people whose sophisticated technologies used the natural resources to ensure their survival, whose military skill might even have prevented European settlement of North America if not for devastating epidemics and disruption of the ecology? Where are the men and women who are today diligently struggling to assert their legal rights and express once again the value of their heritage?

The various Indian tribes of North America, like people everywhere, have a history that includes population expansion, adaptation to a range of regional environments, trade across wide networks, internal strife, and warfare. This was the reality. Europeans justified their conquests, however, by creating a mythical image of the New World and its native people. In this myth, the New World was a virgin land, waiting for the Europeans. The arrival of Christopher Columbus ended a timeless primitiveness for the original inhabitants.

Also part of this myth was the debate over the origins of the American Indians. Fantastic and diverse answers were proposed by the early explorers, missionairies, and settlers. Some thought that the Indians were descended from the Ten Lost Tribes of Israel, others that they were descended from inhabitants of the lost continent of Atlantis. One writer suggested that the Indians had reached North America in another Noah's ark.

A later myth, perpetrated by many historians, focused on the relentless persecution during the past five centuries until only a scattering of these "primitive" people remained to be herded onto reservations. This view fails to chronicle the overt and covert ways in which the Indians successfully coped with the intruders.

All of these myths presented one-sided interpretations that ignored the complexity of European and American events and policies. All left serious questions unanswered. What were the origins of the American Indians? Where did they come from? How and when did they get to the New World? What was their life—their culture—really like?

In the late 1800s, anthropologists and archaeologists in the Smithsonian Institution's newly created Bureau of American Ethnology in Washington,

D.C., began to study scientifically the history and culture of the Indians of North America. They were motivated by an honest belief that the Indians were on the verge of extinction and that along with them would vanish their languages, religious beliefs, technology, myths, and legends. These men and women went out to visit, study, and record data from as many Indian communities as possible before this information was forever lost.

By this time there was a new myth in the national consciousness. American Indians existed as figures in the American past. They had performed a historical mission. They had challenged white settlers who trekked across the continent. Once conquered, however, they were supposed to accept graciously the way of life of their conquerors.

The reality again was different. American Indians resisted both actively and passively. They refused to lose their unique identity, to be assimilated into white society. Many whites viewed the Indians not only as members of a conquered nation but also as "inferior" and "unequal." The rights of the Indians could be expanded, contracted, or modified as the conquerors saw fit. In every generation, white society asked itself what to do with the American Indians. Their answers have resulted in the twists and turns of federal Indian policy.

There were two general approaches. One way was to raise the Indians to a "higher level" by "civilizing" them. Zealous missionaries considered it their Christian duty to elevate the Indian through conversion and scanty education. The other approach was to ignore the Indians until they disappeared under pressure from the ever-expanding white society. The myth of the "vanishing Indian" gave stronger support to the latter option, helping to justify the taking of the Indians' land.

Prior to the end of the 18th century, there was no national policy on Indians simply because the American nation has not yet come into existence. American Indians similarly did not possess a political or social unity with which to confront the various Europeans. They were not homogeneous. Rather, they were loosely formed bands and tribes, speaking nearly 300 languages and thousands of dialects. The collective identity felt by Indians today is a result of their common experiences of defeat and/or mistreatment at the hands of whites.

During the colonial period, the British crown did not have a coordinated policy toward the Indians of North America. Specific tribes (most notably the Iroquois and the Cherokee) became military and political pawns used by both the crown and the individual colonies. The success of the American Revolution brought no immediate change. When the United States acquired new territory from France and Mexico in the early 19th century, the federal government wanted to open this land to settlement by homesteaders. But the Indian tribes that lived on this land had signed treaties with European governments assuring their title to the land. Now the United States assumed legal responsibility for honoring these treaties.

At first, President Thomas Jefferson believed that the Louisiana Purchase contained sufficient land for both the Indians and the white population. Within a generation, though, it became clear that the Indians would not be allowed to remain. In the 1830s the federal government began to coerce the eastern tribes to sign treaties agreeing to relinquish their ancestral land and move west of the Mississippi River. Whenever these negotiations failed, President Andrew Jackson used the military to remove the Indians. The southeastern tribes, promised food and transportation during their removal to the West, were instead forced to walk the "Trail of Tears." More than 4,000 men, woman, and children died during this forced march. The "removal policy" was successful in opening the land to homesteaders, but it created enormous hardships for the Indians.

By 1871 most of the tribes in the United States had signed treaties ceding most or all of their ancestral land in exchange for reservations and welfare. The treaty terms were intended to bind both parties for all time. But in the General Allotment Act of 1887, the federal government changed its policy again. Now the goal was to make tribal members into individual landowners and farmers, encouraging their absorption into white society. This policy was advantageous to whites who were eager to acquire Indian land, but it proved disastrous for the Indians. One hundred thirty-eight million acres of reservation land were subdivided into tracts of 160, 80, or as little as 40 acres, and allotted tribe members on an individual basis. Land owned in this way was said to have "trust status" and could not be sold. But the surplus land—all Indian land not allotted to individuals—was opened (for sale) to white settlers. Ultimately, more than 90 million acres of land were taken from the Indians by legal and illegal means.

The resulting loss of land was a catastrophe for the Indians. It was necessary to make it illegal for Indians to sell their land to non-Indians. The Indian Reorganization Act of 1934 officially ended the allotment period. Tribes that voted to accept the provisions of this act were reorganized, and an effort was made to purchase land within preexisting reservations to restore an adequate land base.

Ten years later, in 1944, federal Indian policy again shifted. Now the federal government wanted to get out of the "Indian business." In 1953 an act of Congress named specific tribes whose trust status was to be ended "at the earliest possible time." This new law enabled the United States to end unilaterally, whether the Indians wished it or not, the special status that protected the land in Indian tribal reservations. In the 1950s federal Indian policy was to transfer federal responsibility and jurisdiction to state governments, encourage the physical relocation of Indian peoples from reservations to urban areas, and hasten the termination, or extinction, of tribes.

Between 1954 and 1962 Congress passed specific laws authorizing the termination of more than 100 tribal groups. The stated purpose of the termination policy was to ensure the full and complete integration of Indians into American society. However, there is a less benign way to interpret this legislation. Even as termination was being discussed in Congress, 133 separate bills were introduced to permit the transfer of trust land ownership from Indians to non-Indians.

With the Johnson administration in the 1960s the federal government began to reject termination. In the 1970s yet another Indian policy emerged. Known as "self-determination," it favored keeping the protective role of the federal government while increasing tribal participation in, and control of, important areas of local government. In 1983 President Reagan, in a policy statement on Indian affairs, restated the unique "government is government" relationship of the United States with the Indians. However, federal programs since then have moved toward transferring Indian affairs to individual states, which have long desired to gain control of Indian land and resources.

As long as American Indians retain power, land, and resources that are coveted by the states and the federal government, there will continue to be a "clash of cultures," and the issues will be contested in the courts, Congress, the White House, and even in the international human rights community. To give all Americans a greater comprehension of the issues and conflicts involving American Indians today is a major goal of this series. These issues are not easily understood, nor can these conflicts be readily resolved. The study of North American Indian history and culture is a necessary and important step toward that comprehension. All Americans must learn the history of the relations between the Indians and the federal government, recognize the unique legal status of the Indians, and understand the heritage and cultures of the Indians of North America.

General James Edward Oglethorpe of Great Britain meets with the Indians of Georgia in this 1734 painting by the Dutch artist Willem Verelst.

BEFORE
THE ENGLISH

At a certain time, the Earth opened in the West, where its mouth is . . . and the Cussitaws [Cussetas] came out of its mouth and settled near by. But the Earth became angry and ate up their children; therefore, they moved.

[T]hey continued their journey and came, in one day, to a red, bloody river. They lived by this river . . . for two years; but . . . it did not please them to remain. They went toward the end of this bloody river, and heard a noise as of thunder. They approached to see whence the noise came. At first, they perceived a red smoke, and then a mountain which thundered; and on the mountain, was a sound as of singing. They went to see what this was; and it was a great fire which blazed upward, and made this singing noise. This mountain they named the King of Mountains. They here met a people of three different Nations [the Chickasaws, the Alabamas, and the Abihkas].

About this time a dispute arose, as to which was the oldest and which should rule; and they agreed, as they were four Nations, they would set up four poles. They would then go to war, and whichever Nation should cover its pole, from top to bottom, with the scalps of their enemies, should be the oldest.

They all tried, but the Cussitaws covered their pole first, and so thickly that it was hidden from sight. Therefore, they were looked upon, by the whole Nation, as the oldest.

The Chickasaws covered their pole next; then the Atilamas [Alabamas]; but the Obikaws [Abihkas] did not cover their pole higher than the knee.

After this they left that place, and . . . came to a people and a town named Coosaw. Here they remained four years. The Coosaws complained that they were preyed upon by a . . . lion.

The Cussitaws said they would try to kill the beast. [And they] killed it with blazing pinewood. They made its bones an important part of their war medicine.

After four years they left the Coosaws. They came to [a] white path, and saw the smoke of a town. This is the place where now the tribe of Palachucolas [Apalachicolas] live.

The Palachucolas . . . gave them white feathers; and asked to have a Chief in common. Since then they have always lived together.

Some settled on one side of the River, some on the other. Those on one side are called Cussitaws, those on the other, Cowetas; yet they are one people, and the principal towns of the Upper and Lower Creeks.

This legend was told to British general James Edward Oglethorpe in 1735 by Chekilli, a Creek headman. The tribe of North American Indians that the British called the Creeks was actually a powerful confederacy of several groups, including the aforementioned Cowetas, Abihkas, and Coosas. The myth that Chekilli recounted, the oldest recorded account of the origin of the Creeks, helps us understand how they came to dwell in the Southeast and how they became a unified group. It also explains much about how the Creeks thought of themselves in the mid-18th century. But it leaves much unanswered, and other sources of information must be used to help fill in the gaps. Some evidence is provided by archaeologists—scientists who study human ways of life in the past through the objects, records, and settlements that people leave behind. These scholars tell us much about how the Creeks lived before the Europeans first arrived in North America.

The ancestors of the Creek Indians lived for hundreds of years in southeastern North America in what are now the states of Georgia and Alabama. They were part of what scholars call the Mississippian culture, so named because it began in the central Mississippi River valley of North America in approximately A.D. 600. By about A.D. 800, Mississippian traditions and practices had spread to Indian groups farther to the south and east. The most visible remains of Mississippian culture are the huge earthen mounds that dot the landscape throughout the southeastern United States. These mounds, which supported temples or the homes of chiefs, were sometimes built as high as 40 to 50 feet. They are the only structures that remain of the many highly organized and flourishing towns of Mississippian society.

The largest of these towns, Cahokia, was the center of Mississippian culture. It was located slightly south of present-day East St. Louis, Illinois, and during its peak in the 13th century may have had more than 10,000 inhabitants. Most Mississippian towns had between 1 and 20 mounds, but Cahokia had at least 100. The largest of them, Monks Mound, still stands and covers more than 1 million square feet.

The Great Temple Mound (right) and Lesser Temple Mound at Ocmulgee National Monument in Georgia. These mounds were constructed by the Mississippian ancestors of the Creeks.

There were no Mississippian towns that large in the Southeast, but some may have been inhabited by as many as 2,000 or 3,000 people. Many of the largest southeastern towns were built around the Mississippian earth mounds, shaped like pyramids with the top cut off. Among the best preserved is Ocmulgee National Monument near present-day Macon, Georgia.

One of the most important characteristics of Mississippian society was its ranked class system, or social hierarchy. Scholars have concluded that such a system existed by studying the burial practices of the Mississippian people. Some corpses were interred with finely carved figurines and ceremonial vessels, jewelry, and other kinds of luxury goods. But others were buried with few objects or none at all. Scholars have concluded that people with lavish grave offerings were probably members of the most powerful class in Mississippian culture—the ruling class.

Scholars also believe that Mississippian society may have had a form of government known as a theocracy, in which the political and religious leaders were one and the same. If this was the case, it would not be unusual in American Indian societies. Indians commonly do not make

A 20th-century artist's conception of a Mississippian village. The traditional daily life of early Creeks in many ways resembled that of their ancestors.

a distinction between religious and secular life, just as they do not believe in the separation of the natural and supernatural worlds. Because religion was a part of every aspect of the Mississippian people's life, scholars believe it is likely that religion would be intertwined with the Mississippian political system and that Mississippian leaders would have handled both ceremonial and political responsibilities.

The Mississippian government was a complex series of social and political organizations known as chiefdoms. The most important aspect of these chiefdoms was their centralization of power. Each chiefdom had one ruler—the chief—who held absolute authority over the people of a particular region. Sometimes a very powerful chief had influence over more than one region. The chiefdom of Coosa, for example, dominated the smaller chiefdoms and communities in what is now northeastern Tennessee through northwest Georgia to central Alabama, a distance of 300 miles. All the people within the range of Coosa's power owed ultimate loyalty to the chief.

The vast mounds of Cahokia and other Mississippian towns provide further evidence to scholars that the Mississippians lived in chiefdoms. Such centralized political power had to exist in order to muster a large enough labor force to build the enormous mounds. The Mississippian people constructed a mound by carrying dirt in baskets to the mound site, where it was dumped in a pile. The job would take hundreds of people many years to accomplish. Scholars believe it would have been impossible to organize such a large group of workers for so long without a strong central government.

Mississippian culture was also notable for its artwork, created in a unique style called the Southeastern Ceremonial Complex. Scholars so named it because they believe that Mississippian artifacts were made as religious emblems, symbols of high office, and tokens of respect for rulers. These artifacts include finely carved and engraved stone and shell necklaces and pendants, stone statues, and intricately wrought stone maces, clubs, and hatchets. The pieces have most often been recovered by archaeologists from graves within the many mounds at Mississippian sites.

The centers of Mississippian society, such as Coosa, began to decline in power sometime during the mid-14th century. Some scholars have suggested that Mississippian towns were becoming overcrowded at this time. One scholar estimated that the population of the region may have reached as high as 6.7 million people. In any case, when Europeans arrived in the Southeast in the early 16th century, they arrived too late to see Mississippian culture at its peak.

The peoples living on the outer edges of the Mississippian territory, however, were not yet greatly affected by the problems of its centers. Therefore, when Spanish explorers traveled among the southeastern Mississippians in the early 1500s, they were impressed by the good-looking people, the large towns, and the prosperous countryside. The Indians who lived there lived well. They had plenty of food, they were strong and healthy, and they did not have to work very hard to survive in the resource-rich region.

One Spanish explorer who traveled through the Southeast and described the Indians living there was Hernando de Soto. In 1539, he landed with an army on what is now the west coast of Florida. Spurred on by the riches other Europeans brought back from Mexico and Peru, de Soto spent more than a year traveling among the ancestors of the Creeks in search of treasure. De Soto did not, however, make a particularly good impression on the Indians of the region. While there, he forced Indian men and women to work, carrying equipment for him, and demanded that Indian towns provide food for his retinue of several hundred men and animals. De Soto also held political and religious leaders, including the chief of Coosa, as hostages so that the Indians would obey his orders.

When Indian warriors resisted his demands, he attacked them with his cavalry. During one daylong battle in the Mississippian chiefdom of Mabila, de Soto's soldiers killed more than 3,000 Indian people. The Spaniards, mounted on horses and protected by armor from the stone-tipped arrows of the Indians, suffered fewer than 150 casualties.

De Soto's march devastated the Indians of the Southeast. In addition to forced labor and warfare, the Europeans brought deadly diseases, such as measles, plague, and smallpox, into their lands. These diseases were common in Europe, and Europeans had developed immunity to them. The sicknesses were unknown in North America, however, and Indian people therefore had no immunity to them. By the tens of thousands they sickened and died. Most scholars now think that within 150 years after Europeans first set foot in the Southeast, their diseases killed between 90 and 95 percent of the Indian population there. One outbreak of an epidemic disease could kill half or more of the inhabitants of an Indian community. And because the people did not understand how the diseases were spread, they often fled to

The front and back of a Mississippian pottery figurine. The piece was found in what was probably a child's grave.

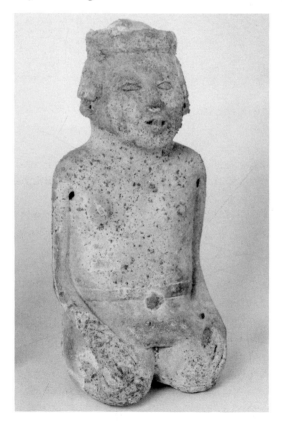 

A 19th-century engraving of the 1539 landing of Spanish explorer Hernando de Soto and his entourage at present-day Tampa Bay, Florida.

the communities of their relatives, carrying the sickness with them. In this way, one European with smallpox could infect an entire region, resulting in the death of thousands of people.

The effects of these epidemics are hard to imagine. Indian people did not have written languages and transmitted orally almost all of their history, religious beliefs, and traditions. When they died, their knowledge died with them. The rapid spread of European diseases killed thousands of people before they were able to pass on their cultural information. Those who survived consequently faced a world nowhere near as rich as it had been before so many of their traditions were lost.

Diseases caused the declining Mississippian chiefdoms to collapse. Surviving Indians abandoned the ceremonial centers and avoided large concentrations of people. Often towns lost most of their population. The survivors from several towns then banded together hoping to flee those areas in which sickness had struck. They tried to recreate their old way of life as best they could, but the loss of so many people and so much knowledge had changed their culture forever.

These Indians often had to create new societies and traditions. The several bands of Indians who make up the Creek Nation probably first came together by this process.

There are no written records detailing the development of Creek culture. The Indians had little contact with Europeans for more than 100 years after the collapse of Mississippian culture in the late 16th century. Because there were no more powerful chiefs or centralized governments, there was no longer any reason for the Indians to create the luxury items sought by European explorers. It was not until the late 17th century that the English began to colonize the region and establish towns and farms. The Indians described by the English settlers were by that time very different from those chronicled by de Soto. In many ways, the Indians were an entirely new people.

Today, many Creeks call themselves Muskogees, the term also used to signify the language that most of them speak. In the late 17th century, however, there were perhaps six distinct languages spoken among the Creeks. At that time, the Creeks did not think of themselves as a people united within a single nation but were instead more like an alliance of independent groups. These groups had joined together for protection after the collapse of the Mississippian culture and the first outbreak of epidemic disease.

In traditional Creek culture, women and men each had particular roles and tasks. Neither group was more important than the other, and each made a vital contribution to the survival of the community. Except for the heavy work, in which they were assisted by the men, women did most of the labor in the fields. Working together in family groups, the women tilled the soil with digging sticks and hoes with points made of bone or sharpened stone. Because it was hard to break the ground with such tools, the Creeks usually lived in river valleys where the soil was loose, rich, and easily worked. Here they planted large plots with corn, beans, squash, and other vegetables.

Rivers also provided the Creeks with fish, an important staple in their diet. Men caught fish with spears and bows and arrows. Creeks also constructed weirs—fences made from woven branches—with which they blocked the path of streams, trapping fish so that they could be more easily caught. Some fish, such as sturgeon, were so large that Indian men would lasso them with vine ropes or dive into the water and wrestle them to the bank. Men sometimes looked for fish in pools of still water along the riverbanks, as well. There they immobilized the fish by poisoning the waters with powders made by pounding certain roots. The poisons stunned the fish but were harmless to the Indians.

Creek men acquired meat during a major hunt for animals that took place in the forests of the Southeast. The animal they most commonly sought was the white-tail deer, but they also hunted other animals, including bears, rabbits, and squirrels. The hunters often burned the undergrowth in the forests in order to encourage growth of the tender grass that deer liked and thereby attract the animals to their territory. They also used fire to drive deer herds into pens where the hunters could kill them more easily. Hunting was hard work, not a sport, and Creek communities depended on their hunters to supply plenty of meat.

Wild plants provided an important supplement to the Creeks' food supply. Women and children gathered herbs, roots, nuts, and berries, as well as special plants, such as button snakeroot, ginseng, and red cedar, known for their medicinal properties.

The Creek people lived in villages, or *Italwas*. They were called towns by the English and came to be commonly known by that term. There was no centralized governing body of the towns because each of them had been founded by independent groups that had separate histories and different customs. Therefore, the town an individual inhabited claimed

A painting by modern-day Creek artist Larry McMurtry of a traditional Creek village.

his or her primary loyalty even though the inhabitants of various towns soon came to share many aspects of their cultures in common.

According to early-18th-century European sources, there were between 50 and 80 Creek towns inhabited by ap-proximately 7,000 or 8,000 people. The towns were geographically divided into two groups—the Upper Towns and the Lower Towns—and most scholars estimate that the Upper Creeks outnumbered the Lower Creeks two to one. The Lower Towns, including the largest,

A plan of a Creek town sketched in the late 18th century by William Bartram, a naturalist who traveled throughout the Southeast and documented many of the Indian cultures there. The sketch includes (A) a chakofa (council house), (B) a town square, (C) a game field, and several Creek family homesteads.

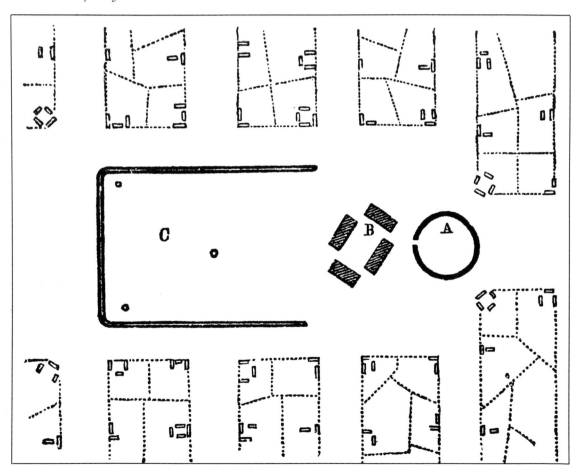

Coweta, were located primarily along the Chattahoochee and Flint rivers in what is now Georgia. The Upper Towns were in what is now Alabama, especially along the Coosa, Tallapoosa, and Alabama rivers and their tributaries. One hundred miles of largely uninhabited land separated the Upper Creeks from the Lower Creeks, and the two groups only occasionally gathered together.

Every major Creek town had a ceremonial and political center called a square ground. The large, open rectangular space was surrounded by long, low buildings with open fronts and seats inside that faced the square. The town leaders sat in these viewing stands during the summer months, when the Creeks entertained foreign dignitaries, held their council meetings, and conducted their religious ceremonies. During the winter, Creek leaders held councils in a communal town house, called a *chakofa* in Muskogee. This building contained the Creeks' ceremonial fire and was located close to the town square. Cone-shaped chakofas were often 30 feet tall, with a base of between 30 and 60 feet in diameter. The larger structures could accommodate up to 500 people.

Most Creeks lived in large family compounds that either surrounded the square ground or spread out for several miles along a stream or river. These compounds consisted of clusters of interspersed gardens, huge fields, and several buildings. The structures included a well-insulated winter house, a smaller version of the chakofa; a summer house, con-

structed of lightly woven poles and sticks; and one or two storage sheds.

Each compound was owned by a family, all the members of which belonged to the same clan—a group of people who consider themselves closely related based on their descent from a common ancestor. Creek clans included the Wind clan, the Bird clan, the Alligator clan, and the Bear clan and varied in size and composition. Clan kin were required to help each other in time of need and to defend or avenge each other when threatened or harmed. Clan membership also determined whom a person could marry. The Creeks considered all clan kin closely related and unsuitable for marriage. Therefore, a Creek had to marry someone from a clan different from his or her own. Clan membership determined just about everything that involved the ways Creek people dealt with each other. A clan gave each individual his or her identity.

The Creek people traced their ancestry through the female line, a practice known as *matrilineality*. Therefore, children belonged to the same clan as their mother. In this system of kinship, children are considered to be related to their mother and all her clan kin but not to their father or his clan kin. Girls learned the skills a Creek woman needed from their mother, who was their clan relative. But a Creek boy would look to his mother's brothers, rather than to his father, to teach him the ways of Creek men. And a Creek father was responsible for the upbringing of his nephews, the sons of his sisters. All Creeks had important roles

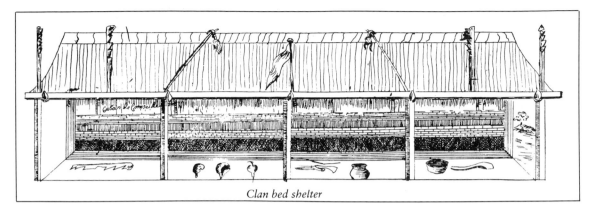

Clan bed shelter

A sketch of a Creek clan shelter from the early 1700s. Creek leaders conducted their business in such buildings, which surrounded the square grounds of Creek towns.

to play, and clan relatives provided their charges with the knowledge they needed to fulfill those roles.

The Creeks also practiced *matrilocality*—after marriage, a young man moved into the compound of his wife and her clan relatives. Even though he lived there, his familial home was with his own clan relatives in another part of the town. Clans controlled the fields and organized the planting and harvesting. Therefore, Creek towns were actually groups of small agricultural communities occupied by groups of clan relatives and the husbands of each clan's married women.

Each Creek town was governed by a chief. In many cases, the leadership position was inherited and always occupied by a member of a specific clan. The chief served as the overseer of all public matters, including the reception of visiting officials, provision of food storage and maintenance, and communication with tribal and non-Indian representatives on behalf of the town. A group of elders and distinguished men of the town made up the town council. They assisted the chief in his duties and decided upon the proper timing for warfare and ceremonies.

Religion was an important part of Creek life. The most significant festival in the Creek year was the annual *poskita*, or Green Corn Ceremony. During this multiday celebration, held in late summer, the Creeks gave thanks for the new corn crop, honored the renewal of life in the new year, and recounted the history and laws of the town. With dance and oratory, they ceremonially cleansed themselves of their misdeeds and forgave others their wrongs.

The most important part of the festival was a ceremony in which the old council fire, kept burning throughout the year, was extinguished by the chief and a new fire was lit. During this time, the women of the tribe extinguished the fires in their home and relit them with embers from the new ceremonial fire. The chief and councilmen also made a ritual drink, known as the Black Drink, that was then ingested by the men of the town. The people also celebrated the ripening of the new corn crop by ritually burning several ears in the new fire.

The two symbolic elements of the ceremony—fire and corn—celebrated life, health, happiness, and the friendship and kinship that united the towns and bound them to one another within the nation. The ceremonial life of the Creeks provided them with a feeling of continuity. But the people of the Creek Nation would soon find little to celebrate. Indeed, in the years to come, invading Europeans would alter the very nature of the bonds that held the Creek people together. ▲

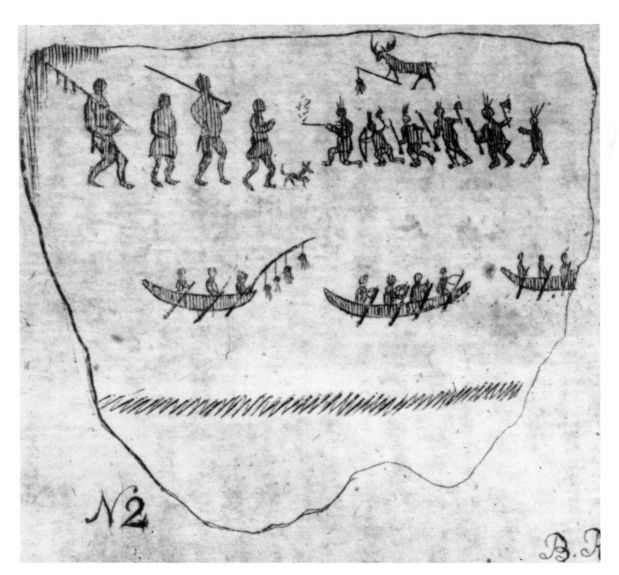

A drawing of pictographs that were carved into a piece of pottery by a Creek war party. The sketch was made by the Dutch botanist Bernard Romans, who in 1775 compiled a natural history of southeastern North America.

TRADE
AND
WAR

During the 100 years between 1570 and 1670 there was probably little or no contact between the Creeks and Europeans. Some Europeans were in the Southeast—the Spanish founded the settlement of St. Augustine in 1565 in what is now eastern Florida, and the English established Jamestown in 1607 on the coast of what is now Virginia. But they either had no dealings with the Creeks or the record of their relations has been lost.

The first English settlement in Creek territory was Charles Town, founded in 1670 by the English as the capital of their colony of Carolina. Both the Creeks and the colonists were anxious to trade with each other, so they soon became well acquainted. Indeed, the English were responsible for the common usage of the name "Creeks." Exactly why the English began referring to the Indians, who referred to themselves by their town

names, by this name is not certain. Most scholars believe, however, that it was because some of the Indians lived at the headwaters of the Ocmulgee River, which was called Ochese Creek during the 17th century. When the traders set out with their goods, they would say they were going to see the Ochese Creek Indians. Eventually, they dropped the name *Ochese* and simply called the Indians Creeks.

The traders wanted two things from the Creeks, deerskins and Indian captives. Merchants in the British colonies shipped the deerskins to England to make leather products and sold the captives to work as slaves in the fields of plantation owners in Carolina and the Caribbean islands. In return, the traders sold the Creeks guns and ammunition, cloth, European-style clothing, beads, paint, metal tools and weapons, copper

British delegations such as this one met often with the Creeks to trade European goods for deerskins, a valuable commodity across the Atlantic.

The Creek warriors' decision to enter the slave trade had terrible consequences. The Creeks, as trading partners of the English, were well armed with guns and ammunition whereas many of the neighboring tribes had few such weapons. Therefore, Creek slave raiders were much more powerful than any of their neighbors. Hungry for English goods, Creek warriors attacked all the nearby tribes. In a short time, the Creeks had entirely wiped out many of these tribes either by killing all their warriors or by capturing for sale everybody they could find. By the 1690s, less than 20 years after trading with the Europeans had begun, only the strongest tribes of the region remained.

As the Creek raiders depleted the supply of captives surrounding their lands, they had to travel farther and farther from home in their quest. At the encouragement of Charles Town leaders, who were anxious to injure their Spanish rivals, Creek raiders in 1704 struck a string of Spanish missions in western Florida and killed or captured an estimated 15,000 Indians living there. Soon after, the Creeks attacked several Choctaw settlements in what is now Mississippi, taking many of the Choctaws as prisoners. The Charles Town merchants did not keep careful records of the captives they purchased from the Creeks, but the number must have been several thousand. For example, a census of Carolina for 1708 listed 1,400 Indian slaves, but scholars have determined that most captured Indians were sold to other colonies.

The trade in human beings caused many changes in the lives of the southeastern Indians. The most drastic effect was the destruction of many tribes that were too small and poorly armed to defend themselves. At the same time, it greatly expanded the wealth, power, and importance of the Creeks. The Charles Town traders kept their main partners well supplied with guns and other imported goods. The Creeks' standard of living was high, and they were the most powerful people in the Southeast.

The position of the Creeks began to change in the early 1700s, however. In 1715 the Yamassees, a tribe living on the Carolina coast south of Charles Town, attacked and killed several hundred settlers. The attack was in retaliation against Charles Town traders who were kidnapping Yamassee women and children to sell in the slave market. The fighting wiped out much of the population of rural Carolina, and the colonial government decided the slave trade in Indian people was to blame. By 1717, colonial forces in Carolina had repulsed the Yamassees and, to assure future peace, the colonial government declared the Indian slave trade illegal. The Creeks, suddenly forced out of the slave business, became wholly dependent on the deerskin trade.

Scholars are not sure how many deer Creek hunters killed for sale to the Charles Town traders. But during the 1740s and 1750s, a period for which good records exist, Charles Town merchants recorded shipping to England a yearly average of 238,000 pounds of skins, representing about 48,000 deer. The Cherokee Indians also sold deerskins to these traders, but reports indicate that goods from Creek hunters accounted for a large percentage of the total. Traders at Savannah, Georgia, shipped an annual average of 156,000 pounds of skins to England between 1755 and 1772, and nearly all of this business was with the Creeks. During much of the 18th century, Creek hunters may have killed for sale as many as 45,000 to 50,000 deer per year.

To nonhunters, this seems a staggering number of deer, but it is an entirely reasonable figure for Creek hunters. Creek men were very good hunters and could easily kill that many deer. European officials estimated that in the mid-18th century the number of adult Creek men ranged between 2,500 and 3,500. If each one of them hunted, he would only have to kill some 15 to 20 deer annually to make up the estimated total.

Scholars are not sure about how much a Creek hunter could buy with his deerskins. The prices that the Indians had to pay for trade goods fluctuated throughout the 18th century, depending on the demand for Indian goods in England and on the distance the traders had to carry the European goods into Indian country. In July 1762, however, the South Carolina colonial commission that regulated trade with the Indians made up a price list for that year that provides an idea of the average cost of particular products. The most expensive item on the list is a saddle and bridle "of the best sort," which cost 20 pounds of deerskin. A gun was almost as expensive at 15 pounds. Gunpowder cost 1 pound of skin for 14 ounces, and 60 bullets cost 1 pound. A small deerskin weighed about 1 1/2 pounds, and a large one could weigh as many as 5 pounds. If a hunter killed 20 deer a year, he had between 30 and 100 pounds of skins to spend.

Creek men had always hunted for deer. But, because of this huge trade in skins, many of them devoted an increasingly large amount of time to hunting. In a sense, they became professional hunters. The Creeks killed so many deer year after year that they soon drastically depleted the deer population of the Southeast. Hunters then had to spend more and more time in the forests looking for deer and travel farther in search of undiscovered herds. Because hunters from other southeastern tribes—the Choctaws and Chickasaws to the west and the Cherokees to the north—were also seeking the animals, Creek hunting parties frequently met foreign hunters in the woods. These chance encounters sometimes ended in bloodshed, as each hunting party considered the other a dangerous competitor for the shrinking number of deer. When conflicts became too serious, they often erupted into war, further disrupting the relations between the Creeks and their neighbors.

As Creek men stayed out hunting for longer periods of time, they neglected many of their responsibilities at home.

Increasingly, Creek women and old men assumed the duties of the absent hunters, and this caused changes in tribal life. The men had been traditionally responsible for the education of Creek boys, for example, and now others had to do so. Decisions on tribal business in the councils and important functions in the many village ceremonies and religious rituals were also delayed. Fortunately, like their Mississippian ancestors, the Creeks were primarily agricultural and the women did the farming. As a result, the long absences of the men did not threaten the people's food supply.

The most important change in Creek society resulting from the deerskin trade was not immediately apparent, however. As their trade relationship with the English grew, the Creeks quickly became dependent on the European market for all the goods they needed. Before the Europeans came, the Creeks were self-sufficient. The men had made their tools and weapons from wood, bone, and stone, and the women had made cooking pots and water jars from clay and clothes from animal skins. The Creeks now bought from the traders manufactured products to replace their handmade goods and, after a few generations, forgot how to make the things they needed. Just as our own society has become dependent on oil, and therefore on the foreign producers of oil, the Creeks became dependent on manufactured goods and the foreign suppliers of those goods.

The Creeks soon faced difficulties as a result of their dependence. Foreign suppliers who wanted to exploit the Creeks'

UPPER AND LOWER CREEK TOWNS

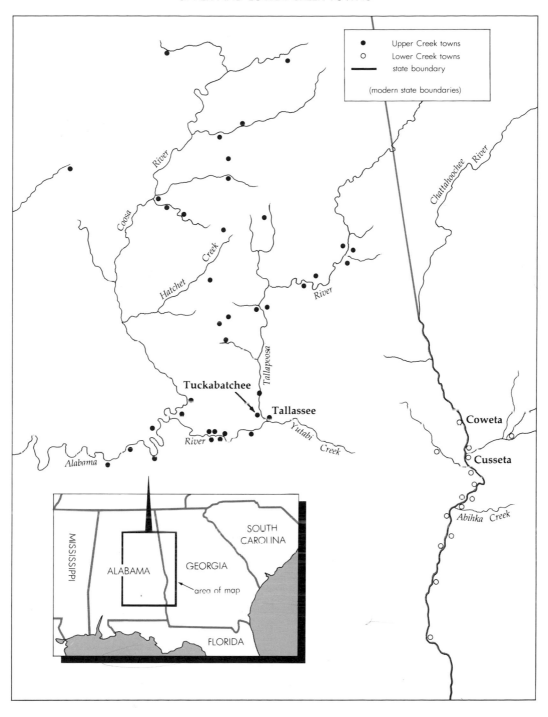

Spanish beads and a coin, used as barter items during trade with the Creeks. The Creeks maintained lucrative trade relationships with the Spanish, the English, and the French during the first half of the 18th century.

situation were able to do so easily by withholding goods or raising prices. European traders did this frequently, each time promising that if the Creeks agreed to do what they wanted, the flow of goods would resume or the prices would be reduced. When the Europeans used this type of pressure, it was hard for the Creeks to resist. They either had to do what they were told or go without the things they needed, which was very difficult. It was especially hard for the Creeks to do without guns and ammunition, because shortages of these items made them vulnerable to their enemies.

The Europeans exerted this kind of economic pressure on the Creeks because of a fierce three-way struggle between

England, France, and Spain for control of the Southeast. The Spanish had been in possession of Florida since 1565 and claimed the whole Southeast as the property of Spain. In 1714, the French moved up the Alabama River from Mobile and built Fort Toulouse, a trading post, among the Upper Creeks near what is now Montgomery, Alabama. And the English had begun to spread down the Atlantic coast into the Southeast soon after they established the colony of Georgia in 1733. All three of these European nations pressured the powerful Creeks to aid them in gaining control of the region.

The Creeks had to decide the best course of action in dealing with these competing forces, but they had a hard time deciding what to do. Many of the Upper Towns were close to Fort Toulouse and supported the French. Many Lower Towns, however, were close to Florida and were friendly to the Spanish. And many of the other towns, both Upper and Lower, traded with the English and supported them. Spokespersons of many of the towns met in a national council at Coweta. The Creek leaders wanted to formulate a policy toward the Europeans, but they could not reach an agreement that was amenable to all and they lacked the power to make or enforce uniform laws that applied to individual towns. The council could not choose to support one European group and force the towns that preferred another to agree with those

terms. The council remained deadlocked until Brims, the chief of Coweta, suggested that the Creeks be friendly to all three European powers. They would trade with them, receive ambassadors from them, and send deputations to them, but ally with none of them against the other powers. If the Creek towns could agree to this, Brims argued, they could remain free and independent. Together they would hold the balance of power in the Southeast.

Early in 1720, the towns agreed to Brims's proposal. The Creeks' decision on diplomacy, along with their large population and their well-armed warriors, enabled them to balance successfully the demands of the three European powers. The Creeks traded with each, allied with none, and held on to their independence for the first half of the 1700s. This diplomacy, along with their large population and their well-armed warriors, made the Creeks the most powerful nation in the Southeast. At the same time, they created a National Council where leaders of the towns met and discussed common problems. While this National Council was by no means a national government with enforcement power over the town, it did permit the Creeks to present a united front to the Europeans and thereby underscore their military power. They would find this power useful when events across the Atlantic Ocean threatened their Nation in the late 1700s. ▲

A 1790 portrait of Hopoithle Mico, leader of the Upper Creek town of Tallassee. In the 1780s, he participated in three controversial treaty negotiations with Georgia state officials.

DIPLOMACY
AND
DEFEAT

During the first half of the 18th century, France, Spain, and Great Britain were locked in a contest for ownership of North America. This rivalry culminated in North America with the French and Indian War, which ended in 1763 in a sweeping victory for Great Britain. The three powers then signed an agreement, the Treaty of Paris (one of several treaties by that name). As the victors of the lengthy conflict, the British gained control of France's lands in Canada and all of Spain's holdings in Florida. As a result, the entirety of the east coast of North America came under the jurisdiction of the British crown.

For the Creeks, this meant the end of the time when they could use diplomacy to maintain their position in the region. There were no longer any French or Spanish traders to compete with the En-glish. Instead, the English in South Carolina, Georgia, and newly acquired Florida now had complete control over the trading economy of the Creeks. More important, the English colonists were aggressive in exploiting their dominance. For the first time in the Creeks' history, they began to feel heavy and concerted pressure by the Europeans on their economy, their government, and their society.

As always, the primary concern of the Creeks after 1763 was to keep European goods flowing into their towns at affordable prices and on honorable terms. At the same time, they struggled to preserve as much of their economic and political independence as possible. In many ways, however, these goals contradicted one another, and the leaders of the Creeks often had to compromise. Tribal leaders were generally good at dealing with Europeans, but with the Spanish and French removed from the Southeast, they could do little to prevent their people's growing dependence on the English.

The most important initial pressure on the Creeks was the increasing number of non-Indians living on their land. When the English began to settle the colony of Georgia in 1733, the Lower Creek headmen had permitted the colonists to occupy a narrow strip of land along the Atlantic coast. The Indians' lands, according to Creek spokesman Malatchie, "by ancient right belong[ed] to the Creek Nation," and the English settlers were only to be allowed a small portion that the Creeks did not use. To make sure that the settlers did what they were told, Malatchie also informed them that Creek warriors had fought "all opposers by War and [could] show the heaps of Bones of their Enemies slain by them in defense of [their] Lands."

During the 1760s and 1770s, however, the population of Georgia grew rapidly— from 6,000 whites and 3,500 black slaves in 1760 to 18,000 whites and 15,000 black slaves in 1773. Made confident by their victory over the French and Spanish, the English soon demanded from the Creeks more land in Georgia and Florida to accommodate their growing numbers. But the Creek population was increasing as well—from some 9,000 in 1732 to perhaps 20,000 in 1772. The Creeks and the settlers in Georgia and Florida were soon competing for land.

The British government soon became fearful that conflicts would arise between settlers and Indians in the southeastern colonies. Therefore, England's king, George III, appointed Edmund Atkin as superintendent of Indian affairs in 1760 to oversee relations between the colonists and the Indians. The British already had such an official in their northeastern colonies who dealt with Indian issues there. A superintendent's job included the regulation of trade, the supervision of purchases of Indian land by colonial officials and settlers, and in every respect the maintenance of peace in the region.

One of the most effective of these superintendents was John Stuart, a former captain in the South Carolina militia, who was appointed to the post in 1761. Under Stuart's direction, British and Creek officials met six times between 1763 and 1773 to discuss problems of mutual concern. Both the Creeks and the colonists wanted to trade, but the two groups disagreed on what the terms of the relationship should be. The Creeks wanted the traders to open stores in their towns and to sell useful goods at fair prices. Many traders, however, wanted to travel through the Indians' country, selling rum to them and charging them prices the Creeks deemed too high. The Creeks also wanted to keep English hunters, cattle raisers, and farmers out of their territory. But the Georgians clamored for more space. They asked the British government to either buy additional territory for them or let them settle where they pleased. Superintendent Stuart often had his hands full trying to keep both the Creeks and the Georgia colonists happy.

A copper engraving published in the 1733 volume Reasons *for Establishing the Colony of Georgia, by Benjamin Martyn. The British government used such idealized images to encourage its citizens to emigrate to North America.*

In order to keep the British at bay, the Creeks sold land to the colonial government for the non-Indian settlers in Georgia and Florida at five of the six conferences. Much of this land had been hunted clean, overgrazed, or otherwise ruined for the Creeks by the Georgia settlers' cattle and hogs. Therefore, the Creeks were willing to sell it for enough money to pay their debts to the traders and to buy more goods. However, these agreements began a trend that over the next several decades would slowly erode the Creeks' political autonomy and independence.

For two decades, Superintendent Stuart worked closely with the Creeks to enforce trade regulations. He also labored diligently to guard their borders in order to prevent Georgia farmers and hunters from illegally entering the Indians' land. Stuart was not always successful. But his efforts to deal fairly with the Creeks and to uphold English laws that protected them won the superintendent the respect and admiration of the Indians. The colonists, on the other hand, were a source of unceasing trouble, and the Indians soon came to hate and fear them. The Creeks found that although many of the English settlers were their enemies, the British king and his officials in the colonies were their friends.

The friendship between the Creek Nation and England was short-lived, however. Troubles between the British government and its colonies had been brewing for some time and in 1776

erupted into the American Revolution, or War of Independence. The colonists wanted the Indian inhabitants of North America to remain neutral during the conflict. The British, however, wanted the tribes to help them crush the rebellion. Each tribe had to determine what action would serve its best interests.

The Creeks' need for manufactured goods was a major factor in their decision. The most important of these goods was gunpowder, and whichever side could supply them with the most had an enormous advantage in attracting Creek sup-

A 1741 woodcut of the British settlement at Savannah. The town was an important trading center from which many Indian goods, such as deerskins, were sent to Europe for sale.

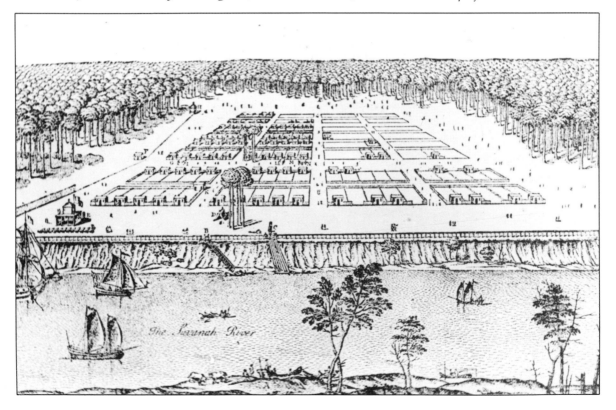

port. The British had more to spare, as well as other goods valuable to the Creeks. Therefore, they had every reason to believe that they could count on the military assistance of the Creeks.

Things were not quite that simple, however. The Creeks had always before remained neutral in the struggle among Europeans and they were reluctant to take sides in the wars of white people in 1776. The Creeks were also frightened by the experience of the Cherokees, their neighbors to the north. The Cherokees had been in direct contact with the southeastern colonists longer than the Creeks and had been very badly treated by them. When Stuart asked them to help the British fight the rebel Americans, the Cherokees enthusiastically agreed and in the summer of 1776 attacked the Carolina frontier. In retaliation, three armies from Virginia and North and South Carolina invaded Cherokee country, burned many towns, destroyed thousands of bushels of corn and other food crops, and drove huge numbers of Cherokees into the mountains as starving refugees.

Many of these Cherokees went to the Creeks for shelter, and their stories of the invasions were terrifying. Representatives from the colonies warned the Creeks that if they attacked, American armies would destroy their country as well. Their threat persuaded the Creeks to remain officially neutral during the revolutionary war. Small parties of Creek warriors sometimes raided colonists' settlements along the Georgia and Florida frontiers, but the Creek Nation made no official alliance with the British. The Creeks continued their old policy of manipulating the balance of power for the duration of the war.

In 1783, the war ended, and the Creeks found themselves in a new and potentially threatening political climate—the colonists had won and had forced the British to withdraw from most of North America. Even more alarming was the news that when the British and Americans made peace in 1783 in the Treaty of Paris, much of the Creek Nation lay within the boundaries of the newly created United States. The Creeks, who considered themselves an independent nation, could not believe that one foreign country presumed to give their territory to another foreign country without their knowledge or consent. As a result of such political upheaval, the Creek leadership had to change its policy toward non-Indians. Instead of concentrating on promoting trade and commerce with whites, they began to concern themselves with defending tribal boundaries and preserving the Nation's independence against the claims of the United States.

During this turbulent period, one of the most important figures in Creek history emerged—Alexander McGillivray. McGillivray was the son of a Creek woman from the influential Wind clan and a Scots trader. Born in about 1762 in the Upper Creek town of Little Tallassee, he was formally educated at schools in Charleston (formerly Charles Town) and Savannah. However, McGillivray's education was interrupted by the outbreak of the American Revolution. He was then appointed by the English to the British

Indian Office as an assistant to Superintendent Stuart and soon became an influential Creek leader.

McGillivray knew that if the Creeks were to be recognized and respected as a sovereign independent nation, they would have to do more than complain about the injustices committed against them by the British and Americans in the 1783 treaty. The main step in asserting the Creeks' sovereignty, McGillivray believed, was the creation of a united Nation under a single government. In the past, the Creeks had always respected the autonomy of their many towns, and their National Council had never attempted to force the towns to follow an overarching policy. This practice had never before been an element of weakness, but the Creeks had never before been so threatened by their non-Indian enemies.

McGillivray's task was not easy, however. He could not impose his ideas on the Creeks—he was not their dictator. But he could use his influence, learning, and experience to convince them that he was right. McGillivray knew that it would take a while for him to effect any change. He decided to buy time by negotiating treaties with both the Americans and the Spanish, thus using the Creeks' time-honored policy of playing one side against the other.

McGillivray first approached the Spanish with a treaty proposal. Using Spain's fear and hatred of the United States, the Creek diplomat struck a deal with the colonial government in the Treaty of Pensacola in 1784. In it, Spain recognized the independence of the Creek Nation and agreed to furnish the Creeks with guns, powder, and other necessary goods. The colonial government also appointed McGillivray as its agent among the Creeks. In return, the Creek Nation promised to act as a buffer zone between the United States and Florida and to keep Americans from Georgia out of Spanish territory.

Well armed with Spanish weapons, McGillivray sent Creek armies east and north to drive Georgia and Tennessee settlers from the Creek Nation. But McGillivray found it was easier to fight American enemies than to convince other Creeks that they needed a strong central government. The politicians who governed many of the Creek towns resented McGillivray and feared that they would lose power if his plan succeeded. Certainly, individual Creek towns would lose their right to form their own policies without regard to the others' interests.

Two influential Creek leaders, Hopoithle Mico (*mico* is the Muskogee word for chief) of Tallassee and Eneah Mico of Cusseta, caused the most difficulty for McGillivray. In an effort to enhance their prestige, the two headmen and some of their followers signed three treaties with representatives of the Georgia state government during the 1780s. McGillivray and his followers denounced the treaties as unauthorized and illegal and gained much popular support for their argument because the documents called for the cession of a large area of Creek land. Most Creeks disapproved of such land sales.

Consequently, in their outrage at the actions of Hopoithle Mico and Eneah Mico, many more Creeks joined McGillivray's faction.

The citizens of Georgia wanted the land ceded to them in the treaty and threatened to take it by force. The state appealed to the U.S. Congress for help because alone it could not come up with enough armed troops to successfully battle Creek warriors armed with Spanish weapons. But the Creek had little to fear from the U.S. government. At that time, Congress was organized under the United States's first constitution, the Articles of Confederation. Under the Articles, the United States had no unified governing body at the federal level. Each

An engraving of a late-18th-century Creek house, from a 1791 drawing by American artist J. S. Tidball.

Benjamin Hawkins, federal agent to the Creeks from 1796 to 1816. Hawkins was responsible for bringing many non-Indian practices to the Creek Nation.

state was responsible for its own defense and upkeep, and thus Congress did not have the power to appropriate funds or soldiers to help Georgia. The powerful Creek warriors under the direction of Alexander McGillivray continued to push the Georgia frontiersmen out of the Indians' land unchallenged.

The Creeks were soon faced with a change in the organization of the U.S. government, however, that would make it more difficult to keep the Georgians at bay. In 1787, delegates from every state except Rhode Island met in Pennsylvania at the Philadelphia Convention. During a series of meetings they drew up and drafted a new set of laws to govern the United States—the Constitution. This document created a strong central government with the power to enforce its policies on the states and their citizens. The framers of the Constitution did for the United States exactly what McGillivray was trying to do for the Creek Nation.

Under the new Constitution, the U.S. government had the authority to raise the money and the armed forces necessary to help Georgia defeat the Creeks. But its first president, George Washington, preferred to establish peace with the Indians. Instead of dispatching an army to Georgia, he sent a diplomat to negotiate with McGillivray and the Creeks. McGillivray agreed to deal with the United States, and in 1790 he led a delegation of Creek leaders to New York, the capital of the United States at the time, to sign a treaty. In this treaty the United States recognized the sovereign independence of the Creek Nation, acknowledged that the land cessions made by Hopoithle Mico and Eneah Mico were unauthorized and illegal, approved McGillivray's plan for improving trade relations, and promised to protect the boundaries of the Creek Nation from encroachment by American citizens. In

The first page of the Articles of Confederation of the United States. The document, written right after the War of Independence, was the predecessor of the U.S. Constitution.

return, the Creeks sold to the United States a 3-million-acre block of land for Georgia.

In a secret addition to the treaty, the U.S. president made McGillivray a brigadier general in the U.S. Army. The appointment, which allowed McGillivray access to top-level decision making, was kept secret so as not to endanger the Creek Nation's relationship with Spain.

McGillivray considered the treaty a great success. By recognizing Creek sovereignty and promising to protect the borders of the Nation, the United States had agreed to support the two main goals of Creek national policy. Like the 1784 treaty with Spain, the 1790 treaty with the United States went a long way toward giving McGillivray the time he needed to complete his political revolution at home. If he could succeed there, he believed, the future of the Creek Nation would be secure.

Unfortunately for the Creeks, McGillivray died in 1793 at the age of 34 before his plans were completed. His death left the Nation in turmoil. Confusion increased with Georgia's unwillingness to respect the 1790 treaty and with the refusal of the U.S. government to force the state to observe its terms. Instead, Washington's administration launched a policy of trying to make the Creeks adopt the culture of whites and acculturate them to mainstream American society.

In 1796, President Washington appointed Benjamin Hawkins, a former congressman from North Carolina, as the southeastern Indian superintendent. Hawkins was to enforce Washington's policy in the area. Like McGillivray, he wanted the Creeks to have a strong centralized government. The two men differed, however, as to the goals of such a government. McGillivray wanted an official body to preserve and protect the land and sovereignty of the Creeks, whereas Hawkins wanted a tool that he could control to enforce U.S. government policies.

During Hawkins's two decades among the Creeks he enjoyed some success in implementing the destruction of the traditional Creek system of government. He subdivided the Nation into legislative districts and established a system for appointing representatives to the Creek National Council. He also encouraged the Council to create an executive committee and appoint a national police force, known as the lawmenders, to arrest and punish those tribemembers who violated Creek law.

With this political system in place, Hawkins urged the Creeks to permit missionaries to enter the Nation. He wanted them to establish schools and begin to instruct Creek children in the Christian religion, the English language, mathematics, and mainstream American agricultural and social practices. At the same time, Hawkins introduced cotton and European-style farm implements and tools and encouraged cattle and hog raising. He worked especially closely with those few Creeks who had already begun to own black slaves, to build non-Indian types of houses, and to buy and sell goods in the markets of Georgia and Tennessee. In these and other ways, Hawkins was trying to induce the Creeks to live like the frontier farmers of the neighboring states.

To succeed in his plan, however, Hawkins had to reverse the roles that Creek culture ascribed to men and women. Women had always been the farmers in Creek society, but Hawkins insisted that the men should assume these tasks, just as men did in non-Indian society. Women, he believed, should stay in the home and cook, clean, make cloth and clothes, and raise children. Both Creek men and women resisted these revolutionary changes in their society, but many slowly began to follow the examples of Hawkins, the missionaries, and the Creek families in which the husband/father was white.

Many Creeks altered their way of life to ward off economic disaster. As the market for deerskins declined, they needed other sources of revenue to keep goods flowing into the Nation. The Creeks sold two more tracts of land on their eastern border in 1802 and 1805, but these sales did not generate enough revenue to last long. Reluctantly, many Creeks adopted the style of living encouraged by Hawkins, essentially commercial agriculture, in order to survive.

Most of the Creeks who adopted non-Indian ways were from the Lower Towns in the eastern part of the Nation near Georgia. Among the Upper Creeks, who lived in the western portion, there were

A portrait of Tecumseh, the Shawnee war leader and prophet.

few converts. The result was that the old factional conflicts that had always characterized Creek politics took on a new, cultural dimension that pitted many Lower Creeks and Upper Creeks against one another. Indeed, by 1810, serious trouble was brewing in the Creek Nation. The Upper Creeks resented the culture changes among the Lower Creeks and

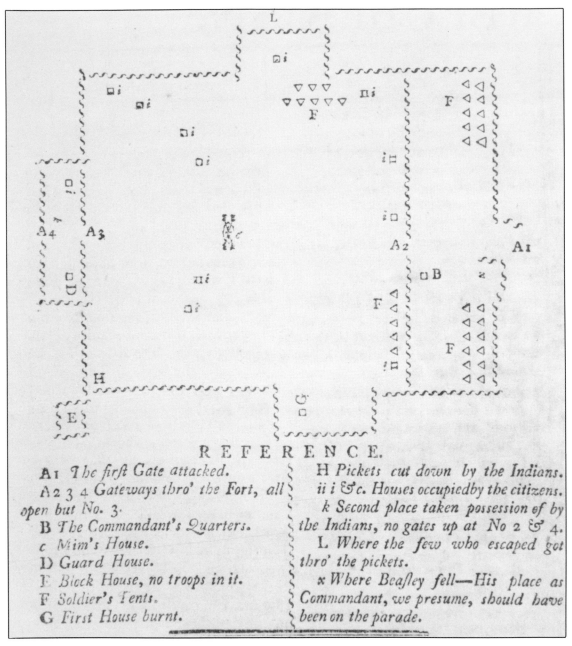

REFERENCE.

A1 The first Gate attacked.
A2 3 4 Gateways thro' the Fort, all open but No. 3.
B The Commandant's Quarters.
c Mim's House.
D Guard House.
E Block House, no troops in it.
F Soldier's Tents.
G First House burnt.

H Pickets cut down by the Indians.
ii i &c. Houses occupied by the citizens.
k Second place taken possession of by the Indians, no gates up at No 2 & 4.
L Where the few who escaped got thro' the pickets.
x Where Beasley fell—His place as Commandant, we presume, should have been on the parade.

A plan of Fort Mims. The Creeks' attack on the fort provided President Andrew Jackson with the final excuse for removing the tribe to Indian Territory.

feared that they would be increasingly pressured to abandon their traditions as well. They wanted to remain Creeks and not become imitations of white people.

Because of these fears, the Upper Creeks resisted the U.S. government's efforts to build a highway, called the Federal Road, through their country. The Lower Creeks had agreed to its construction in a treaty in 1805, but the Upper Creeks felt that if they permitted white people to cross the Indians' country with their families, their herds, and their slaves, the intruders would kill their game, cut their trees, foul their water, sell whiskey to their young people, and want to stop and settle. The whites would cause trouble and the American government would use it as an excuse to demand more land. In the face of this resistance, Hawkins had to use political pressure to see that the road was built.

The mounting assaults on the Indians' lands and culture increased the anxieties of the Upper Creeks, leaving them unsure of themselves and vulnerable. Into the midst of this turmoil came Tecumseh. The Shawnee war leader was traveling among the Indians of the eastern United States, attempting to unite them in fighting to hold back the onrushing tide of white American settlers.

In the fall of 1811, Tecumseh and his retinue spent a week in Tuckabatchee, the main Upper Creek town, during which he urged the tribespeople to join in his revolution. He preached that Indians should rise up against the intrusive white race. He then returned home but

left behind a few missionaries to teach the Creeks his religious message.

A small number of Upper Creek warriors, principally from the westernmost town of Koasati, accompanied Tecumseh to his home in Shawnee territory. The warriors spent the winter in west central Ohio among the Shawnee and returned home in the spring of 1812. On their way back, the warriors encountered some white settlers in western Tennessee and, under the sway of Tecumseh's message, murdered them. The act enraged the governor of Tennessee, Willie Blount, who wrote to Secretary of War John Armstrong demanding retaliation against the Creeks.

Superintendent Benjamin Hawkins was quickly instructed by Secretary Armstrong to arrest the murderers. At Hawkins's insistence, Creek leaders sent out the lawmenders to bring them back, but the police killed them instead. The friends and relatives of the warriors were outraged. Now, they said, Creek leaders were killing their own people to please Hawkins and the U.S. government. All the fears, anxieties, and frustrations that had built up among the Creeks for the past 15 years came to a head.

In order to ward off the impending destruction of the Creek Nation, a group of Creek prophets, known as the Red Sticks, including Josiah Francis (Hillis Hadjo), High-head Jim (Cusseta Tustunnuggee), Paddy Walsh, and Peter McQueen, emerged to lead the embittered Upper Creeks. The group consisted of those who had opposed the Federal

Road, had grievances against white squatters, and feared the Creeks' growing dependence on American goods. These Indians resisted forced cultural change and were angered by their political leaders, who did the bidding of Superintendent Hawkins even when it meant killing fellow Creeks. Two-thirds to three-fourths of the Upper Creeks united behind the prophets, demonstrating the depth of the Indians' disaffection.

The message of the prophets was simple. The Creeks had to return to traditional ways, sever all economic ties with Americans, and expel whites and mixed-blood Creeks who lived like whites. They also had to overthrow those leaders who were more responsive to Hawkins than to their own people, such as Big Warrior (Tustunnuggee Thlucco), a friend of Hawkins's, and the leader of Tuckabatchee, whom the prophets considered their main Upper Creek enemy.

By the spring of 1813 the prophets and their followers had gained enough strength to strike out against Big Warrior and other Creeks influenced by American ways. Burning plantations and killing cattle and hogs, they terrorized the region and drove those who could escape into newly fortified Tuckabatchee, where Big Warrior had gathered a huge supply of corn to feed the refugees. Surrounded by the prophets' army, Big Warrior sent to Hawkins for help. Hawkins was anxious to crush the prophets, whom he denounced as reactionary enemies of peace and of his policies of Americanization. Therefore, he immediately sent a rescue

party of Lower Creek warriors, mostly from Cusseta and Coweta, led by a powerful Coweta headman, William McIntosh. The group broke through the lines of the prophets' army, rescued the beleaguered people trapped in Tuckabatchee, and led them to safety across the Chattahoochee River into Lower Creek country.

It is not known if the prophets intended to invade the Lower Creeks, but they did send a party to Pensacola, Florida, to acquire gunpowder from the Spanish. Laden with the powder, the warriors stopped on their way home at Burnt Corn Creek, in what is now southern Alabama. While they were resting, a party of white settlers and mixed-blood Creek planters from nearby Pensacola attacked them and confiscated the powder. The prophets mounted a counterattack in the summer of 1813. Their target was Fort Mims, a fortified plantation in southwestern Alabama that was owned by a retired trader. The fort was occupied by some 300 people, of whom some were white but most were families of mixed-blood Creeks. Some inhabitants had participated in the attack on the prophets at Burnt Corn Creek. The Creeks at Fort Mims were also hated by the prophets for their collaboration with whites. The prophets' army greatly outnumbered the defenders of Fort Mims, and the invasion was well planned. When the battle was over, nearly all the occupants of the fort, about 260 people, were dead.

The slaughter at Fort Mims changed everything. Until this time, the white in-

A beaded pouch that belonged to a Creek warrior. It was taken from its owner by a U.S. soldier during the Battle of Horseshoe Bend.

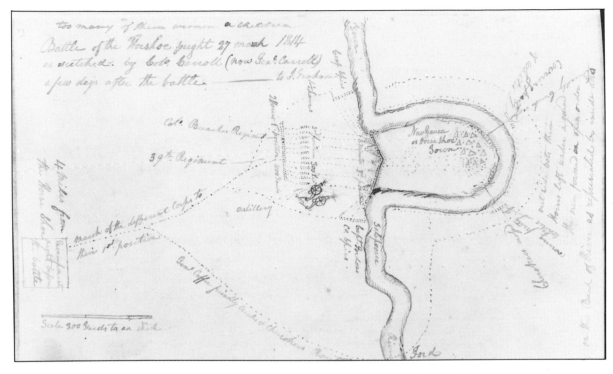

A map of the battlefield at Horseshoe Bend, sketched in 1814 by Colonel William Carroll. Included are the positions of the U.S. Army regiments (cannons) and the Indian encampment (triangles).

habitants of the Southeast had considered the Creeks' battles among themselves an internal, civil conflict and not the business of any outsiders. The events at Fort Mims, however, were more than the settlers could stand. Many white people had been killed there, and their deaths required revenge. More important, the people of Tennessee, Georgia, and Mississippi saw the attack as a perfect excuse to mount armies, invade the Creek Nation, and steal millions of acres of prime cotton land. No one could object, because the Creeks could be blamed for starting the warfare. Furthermore, many whites believed that the Creeks were allies of the British, with whom the United States was again battling in the War of 1812 (1812–15). Armies of white settlers invaded the Creek Nation from three sides—east, north, and west. The largest number of troops came from Tennessee, led by General Andrew Jackson.

Between the late summer of 1813 and the spring of 1814, the three armies, aided by William McIntosh and his Lower Creek forces, rampaged through the Upper Creek country burning towns and killing people. The conflict ended in March 1814 along the Tallapoosa River in a skirmish known as the Battle of Horseshoe Bend. As a result of the war, more than 3,000 Creeks (about 15 percent of the total population) lost their lives, and much of the Upper Creek country was left as barren as the moon.

In August 1814, General Jackson dictated the terms of a peace treaty. The main feature of the document, known as the Treaty of Fort Jackson, was the surrender without payment of 25 million acres of Creek land in central Alabama and southern Georgia. The scheme of the nearby settlers had worked perfectly. For the first time in its history, the Creek Nation had been successfully invaded and defeated and its armies shattered. The Creek people had been so impoverished by the devastating war that they could never again pose a military threat to the South. And a huge tract of valuable land was now available for white settlement.

More than 50 years had elapsed since 1763, when the Creeks were presented with a new political order in the Southeast. For a time they had been able to adapt their strategy of staying neutral and using diplomacy to dictate the balance of power, but this practice was no longer enough. With the independence of the United States and the establishment of the constitutional government, the Creeks were faced with a single enemy who rapidly became more powerful, rich, and aggressive. And this enemy would prove even more aggressive than the Creeks had ever imagined in the years after their defeat at Horseshoe Bend. ▲

Creek leader William McIntosh negotiated the illegal Treaty of Indian Springs with U.S. representatives on February 12, 1825. He was later executed by the Creek Nation for the deed.

4

STRUGGLE
FOR
AUTONOMY

The aftermath of the Treaty of Fort Jackson left the Creek Nation in a difficult and unfamiliar position. For the first time in their history, the Creeks were not more powerful than their enemies. Still worse, the number of their enemies was growing much faster than the Indians' own population. Between 1815 and 1820, settlers poured through the Creek Nation heading for the lands in Mississippi and in Alabama ceded by the Creeks in the treaty. In 1810, the census for Alabama listed 9,000 non-Indians; in 1820, the figure rose to 128,000. Most of the newcomers settled in the ceded territory. The loss of so much rich land simply made harder the already difficult job of recovering from the massive property losses suffered by the Creeks during the 1813–14 war. The invading armies had burned the Indians' towns and homes, confiscated or destroyed their crops and cattle, and generally devastated the land. Never before had the Creeks been so beaten, so poor, and so weak. And never before had their future looked so bleak.

While Creek families set to work rebuilding their lives and homes, two men rose to positions of power and authority. They soon set into motion a political conflict that, in some ways, remains to this day an important issue in Creek public life. One was David B. Mitchell, a former governor of Georgia, whom President James Madison appointed to the post of federal agent (previously known as superintendent) to the Creeks after the death of Benjamin Hawkins in 1816. Throughout his political career, Mitchell had been a leading figure in Georgia's fight to acquire for its citizens all the land belonging to the Indians within its bor-

David B. Mitchell, former governor of Georgia, was appointed federal agent to the Creeks in 1816. He immediately set out to undermine the Creeks' sovereignty and to take from them all of their lands in Georgia by whatever means necessary.

ders. Therefore, friends of the Creeks were appalled by his new appointment, which was like letting the fox into the chicken coop. William Baldwin, a navy surgeon who knew Mitchell, stated, "I . . . cannot entertain a doubt that . . . he will lean to the side of Georgia—the state where he is *popular*, and where the *popular* cry is—*exterminate the savages.*" Indeed, Mitchell immediately set out to undermine Creek sovereignty through bribery of public officials and other forms of corruption.

The other influential man to rise to prominence was powerful Lower Creek leader William McIntosh, who was Mitchell's main ally and henchman. In 1813, Benjamin Hawkins had chosen McIntosh to lead the war party that rescued Big Warrior from the Creek prophets' attack, and he had continued to gain power since that time. Born in the 1770s of a Creek mother and a Scottish father, McIntosh grew up in Coweta, the most important Lower Creek town. He was a member of the influential Wind clan, spoke English well, and by about 1805 had become an important member of Coweta's town council. For his alliance with the United States during its wars with the Creeks, the Coweta leader received from President Andrew Jackson the rank of brigadier general.

Soon after the Treaty of Fort Jackson, McIntosh was named speaker of the Lower Creek council and, because head chief Little Prince (Tustunnuggee Hopoie) of the Lower Creeks was very old and feeble, he assumed an important position in Lower Creek affairs. Indeed, between 1805 and 1820 he attended three negotiating sessions with the U.S. government in Washington. Because he could speak English well, he was the man with whom the government commissioners most often spoke during meetings. The U.S. representatives did not know how the Creek government worked, and it was easy for them to misunderstand McIntosh's position and conclude that he was the sole leader of the Lower Creeks.

McIntosh and agent Mitchell were partners in various business deals, including a store located in the heart of the Creek Nation, on the west bank of the Chattahoochee River. Many people charged that the partners cheated the Creeks who shopped there. McIntosh and Mitchell also controlled the distribution of the annual payment, called an annuity, of several thousand dollars a year owed to the Creeks by the United States for previous land sales. Some Creek leaders thought the money should be placed in a national treasury, but McIntosh and Mitchell illegally used it to pay the inflated debts owed to their store by individual Creeks.

The Creeks' troubles with Mitchell ended in 1821 when a federal investigation found him guilty of participation in the illegal smuggling of Africans into the United States to be sold as slaves. Under Mitchell's direction, the slave traders brought captives into the United States from Spanish Florida by way of the Creek Nation. After Mitchell's conviction, Secretary of War John C. Calhoun fired him, and President James Monroe replaced him with one of Alabama's representatives to Congress, John Crowell. Crowell came on the scene with two of his brothers, both of whom opened stores and taverns that competed with the store owned by McIntosh and Mitchell. Crowell further threatened McIntosh's power by refusing to let him continue to control the distribution of the annuity. McIntosh was angered by these changes and soon became locked in a power struggle with Crowell, who was backed by Upper Creek headman Big Warrior (Tustunnuggee Thlocco). Big Warrior had long been resentful of McIntosh's power among the Lower Creeks, but as long as Mitchell had

been Creek agent, there had been nothing he could do about it. With Mitchell gone, Big Warrior threw his support behind Crowell, and together they worked to push McIntosh aside.

During the early 1820s, the legislature of Georgia began to increase its demands for more Creek land cessions. According to the terms of a special agreement signed in 1802 between the United States and Georgia, the federal government was obligated to purchase and hand over to Georgia all the lands owned by Indians in the state. But after nearly 20 years, the Creeks still owned western Georgia, and the Cherokees still held the northern half of the state. Growing impatience among the settlers in Georgia for that land became a hot political issue. Georgia's politicians began to demand that the U.S. government fulfill its promise. The government maintained that it was doing all it could, but because the 1802 agreement specifically recognized the right of the Indians to refuse to sell, there was nothing it could do to force them out, legally or morally. The Monroe administration agreed to try again, however, and in 1821 succeeded through bribery in buying half of the Creeks' land remaining in Georgia. McIntosh and a handful of other prominent Lower Creek headmen received a great deal of money, perhaps $40,000 to McIntosh alone, and several valuable tracts of land in Georgia. But instead of satisfying the Georgians' pleas for land, the acquisition simply whetted their appetites for more. Thus, beginning in the early 1820s, the pressure on the Creeks to give up their territory and get out of Georgia increased at an alarming rate. The issue was debated in Congress and discussed by the president's cabinet, and it became the main focus of Georgia state politics.

With all hope for military defense destroyed, the Creeks had to figure out new ways to resist and survive. They turned now to political and diplomatic solutions, but this decision required them to make radical changes in their system of government. The Creek Nation had always been a loose alliance of independent towns whose leaders met periodically in the Creek National Council. During such times, they discussed matters of common interest, but the Council was not a legislature that could pass laws, and there was no executive branch with the power to enforce its will. Everything depended on voluntary agreement among the Creek leadership. Without that, there was no political unity.

The Creeks did have some ideas, however, about changing their government to suit the situation in which they found themselves. In the 1780s and 1790s, Alexander McGillivray had talked of these problems and had tried to establish a unified national government. And Benjamin Hawkins had helped them develop judicial districts and create the lawmenders to enforce the Nation's laws. Furthermore, the Creeks' neighbors to the northeast, the Cherokees, were experimenting with political centralization, and there was much to be learned from them.

The actual events surrounding the creation of the Creeks' national government are unclear, but enough important facts are known to provide an idea of what happened. In 1818, the National Council convened and enacted a written code of laws. The most important of these defined the boundaries of the Nation and declared that all the land contained therein was national domain. The territory could not be sold without the expressed authorization and approval of the Council on pain of death. Indeed, the Creek leaders nearly executed William McIntosh in 1821 for his part in a land cession that year, and only his fast talking and the Council's reluctance to kill so prominent a leader saved his life. Moreover, Big Warrior was actively working with Agent Crowell to undermine McIntosh's power so that leadership would be concentrated in his own hands. During the early 1820s, two well-educated young Cherokees, John Ridge and David Vann, spent considerable time among the Upper Creeks serving as their advisers and clerks.

One of the most significant events occurred in late 1823 when McIntosh, employed by two Georgians serving as U.S. treaty commissioners, went among the Cherokees with money to bribe the Cherokee leaders into selling their country and moving west. The Cherokee Council learned of McIntosh's activities, expelled him from the Nation, and wrote a letter to the Creek Council describing what had happened and warning the Creeks "to keep a strict watch over [McIntosh's] conduct, or if you do not he will ruin your Nation."

During the next year, Georgia used its political power to convince Congress to appoint a team of federal commissioners to negotiate a treaty with the Creeks that would provide for tribal land cessions and their relocation, or removal, elsewhere. At the same time, McIntosh was trying to erase the bad impression the National Council had of him after the Cherokee affair by reaffirming his commitment to the law that forbade unauthorized land sales. Meanwhile, the National Council held a series of special meetings and mapped out a strategy to resist a movement afoot in Georgia and Washington to exert further pressure on the Creeks to move west. In two statements they had published in Georgia newspapers, the Creek leaders announced that "on no account whatever will we consent to sell one foot of our land." Furthermore, they reminded all Creeks of their law prohibiting unauthorized land sales. "We have a great many chiefs and headmen but, be they ever so great, they must all abide by the laws. We have guns and ropes: and if any of our people break these laws, those guns and ropes are to be their end." Big Warrior (head chief of the Upper Creeks), Little Prince (head chief of the Lower Creeks), and several Council chiefs signed the document. The warning to chiefs "ever so great" suggests that they were thinking of McIntosh.

This was a critical period in Creek history. The National Council had decided

Cherokee David Vann served as a clerk and adviser to the Upper Creek leadership during the early 1820s.

to resist the efforts of Georgia and the United States to expel the Creeks from their land. The Creeks still had a sovereign right to refuse the sale of their land no matter how badly Georgia and the United States wanted it. But all the Creeks, especially the leaders, had to agree to the policy for it to succeed. Although the Nation had a law that forbade an unauthorized land sale and sentenced to death anyone who disobeyed it, the Council had never actually enforced it. In fact, the Council had never actually carried out any law that applied to relations within the Nation. The only laws that the lawmenders had dealt with related to crimes by Creeks against whites. In other words, the Council had never actually acted as a national government, and none of the leaders knew exactly what to expect from their creation.

On December 7, 1824, the U.S. treaty commissioners opened negotiations with the Creek headmen at Broken Arrow, the hometown of Little Prince. The president had instructed the commissioners to demand that the Creeks sell all their land in the East. The federal government's hope was that with no land left the Creeks would have to leave the country and resettle on as yet undetermined lands set aside for them west of the Mississippi River. The government would pay several hundred thousand dollars for the land in the East, pay all moving expenses, provide food for one year to afford the Creeks time to harvest their first crop, and pay a small amount to each adult for his or her trouble. In addition, the government would give compensation for any land improvements, such as houses, plowed fields, fences, and orchards that the Creeks left behind.

The headmen, of course, vigorously rejected the plan. Big Warrior's speaker, Opothle Yoholo, announced the decision of the chiefs, saying he "would not take a house full of money" for Creek land. The headmen expected their rejection to end the talks, but McIntosh invited the commissioners to his tavern at Indian Springs, where he told them he would sell all the lands in Georgia if the price was right. The commissioners hurried back to Washington to get permission to deal with McIntosh alone. They told the president that McIntosh was so important he could get away with it and that it was the best deal the United States could get. It would not mean the total removal of the Creeks from the East, but at least they would be forced to leave Georgia. President Monroe refused to authorize a treaty signed only by McIntosh for the Georgia land alone, but the commissioners returned to Indian Springs, and they and McIntosh cemented the deal anyway. The document that the participants drafted and signed on February 12, 1825, called the Treaty of Indian Springs, thus violated both Creek national law and the explicit orders of the president.

The treaty was very damaging for the Creek Nation. It required them to sell all their land in Georgia, which belonged to the Lower Creeks, and two-thirds of their land in Alabama, the region of the Upper Creeks. In return, the Creeks would receive $400,000 plus all the removal benefits rejected in December at Broken Arrow. McIntosh and a few hundred of his associates, a small percentage of the roughly 20,000 Creeks, would receive half of the cash payment. McIntosh also received the exorbitant sum of $25,000 for his tavern and two tracts of his private lands at Indian Springs.

When McIntosh signed the treaty, he knew he could be signing away his life. Creek chief Opothle Yoholo, who was present at the meeting but refused to sign the treaty, cautioned McIntosh: "My friend, you are about to sell our country; I now warn you of your danger!" McIntosh did not need the warning. He knew full well that his actions were in violation of Creek national law and that the Council could order his execution. Afraid they might do so, McIntosh took steps to preserve his life. At his insistence, the U.S. commissioners inserted a clause in the treaty requiring the United States to protect him from the vengeance of the Creek National Council. Governor

The Indian Spring Hotel, built by William McIntosh in 1823. The Butts County Historical Society of Georgia is currently restoring the historic landmark to its original appearance.

Georgia governor George M. Troup was adamantly opposed to the continued presence of the Creeks in his state. He demanded that the U.S. government fulfill the terms of the illegal Treaty of Indian Springs.

George M. Troup of Georgia, of whom McIntosh's Scottish father was an uncle, also promised him protection. Believing his life to be adequately safeguarded, McIntosh signed.

Upon hearing of McIntosh's illegal treaty, the National Council immediately sent protests to Washington in the hope of blocking its ratification by the U.S. Senate. In the meantime, the Council stripped McIntosh of his rank and offices. In mid-April, the Council was astonished to learn that despite overwhelming evidence of its illegality, the treaty had been ratified. They also learned that Governor Troup was preparing to send state surveyors into the Creeks' lands in Georgia to mark them off for distribution to Georgia settlers. The Council acted quickly. In a secret session the headmen pronounced McIntosh, his sons-in-law Samuel and Benjamin Hawkins (a Creek man, not the former agent), and Etomme Tustunnuggee guilty of violating national law and ordered their execution. On the afternoon of April 29, a force of nearly 200 Creek lawmenders under the command of former Red Stick leader Menawa of Okfuskee left for McIntosh's home, Lockchau Talofau. The following day they arrested and executed McIntosh, Etomme Tustunnuggee, and Samuel Hawkins. They shot and wounded Benjamin Hawkins, but he escaped with his life. The traitors had been dealt with successfully, but the treaty that they signed would prove more difficult for the Creeks to overcome.

The betrayers of the Creek Nation had provided the catalyst for the creation of a unified Creek government that was now well prepared to fight for its land. The Europeans who came to settle in Creek country were latecomers, and it was simply unreasonable to the Creeks that these interlopers could lay claim to the Creek Nation. Opothle Yoholo expressed those sentiments best, stating, "If the Georgians wanted the Creeks' lands so badly they were willing to kill all the Creek people to get it, then let them come, and the Creeks would die in their homeland. But they would not leave." When the Council passed the law against the unauthorized sale of land, it made clear that the Nation belonged to all the Creek people, and no individual or small group could dispose of it without the approval of all. In this way the Creek National Council became a unified power, and with this power the Creeks expected to defend their lands and their property. However, events to come would prove them wrong. ▲

Opothle Yoholo, speaker of the Upper Creek council, was one of the Creeks' most important leaders during the removal era.

EXPULSION
FROM
THE SOUTHEAST

The 1825 execution of William McIntosh horrified and enraged the Georgia state authorities. To them, the act of the Creek lawmenders was evidence of the Indians' "savagery." Georgia's governor George Troup was especially outraged by the "murder" of his cousin because he feared that the Georgians would now be endangered if they attempted to occupy the lands ceded illegally in the Treaty of Indian Springs. Agent Crowell, along with Opothle Yoholo, Big Warrior, and the other Creek leaders, all tried to reassure the federal government in Washington that McIntosh had been legally executed as a traitor to his nation and that the Creeks had no plans to invade Georgia. But they also made it clear that the Council would not honor the terms of the treaty and that the Creeks would not withdraw from their lands east of the Chattahoochee River without a fight.

President John Quincy Adams, inaugurated while the Senate was ratifying the Treaty of Indian Springs, was extremely eager to avoid bloodshed between the Creeks and the Georgia settlers. He therefore sent a fact-finding mission headed by General Edmund P. Gaines to consult with both Governor Troup and the Creek National Council. The president hoped that once tempers had cooled, the Creeks would reevaluate their situation and quietly accept the treaty terms.

However, after completing his study, General Gaines quickly adopted the view of the Creek Council that the Indian Springs treaty was fraudulent. He reported to President Adams that it would take an army to oust the Creeks and it would be wrong to do so. He recommended that the president let the Georgians stew awhile. After all, they had caused all the trouble from the beginning with their aggressive plans to expel the Creeks and steal their land. He expressed the opinion that as long as the Creeks remained peaceably within their boundaries, they should be left alone.

Of course, Governor Troup and Georgia's congressional delegation refused to settle for this plan and demanded that the terms of the treaty be fulfilled. Troup called together the Georgia militia and distributed weapons, and for a brief period in 1825 President Adams feared that a war would erupt. To calm the situation, save lives, appease the Georgians, and extricate himself from a serious political crisis, Adams suggested that another treaty be negotiated with the Creeks. He planned to ask the Creek headmen to agree to a fair cession of the lands claimed by Georgia. If the Creeks approved the sale, the United States would agree to rescind its claims to the large block of land ceded in the Treaty of Indian Springs that lay west of the Chattahoochee River and included most of the Upper Creek towns.

At this time, new leadership was in place in the Creek Nation. Big Warrior had died, and Little Prince was too aged to be an effective leader. Opothle Yoholo emerged as the unofficial leader of the Creeks, even though he was only the speaker for the Upper Creek Council. He and the other headmen of the Creek Nation agreed to Adams's suggestion. In November 1825, a delegation of headmen led by Opothle Yoholo traveled to Washington to oversee the negotiations.

The talks were lengthy, largely because the Creeks initially refused to sell any land west of the Chattahoochee River. The Creek headmen knew that the Georgia settlers would never respect a surveyed boundary line and therefore insisted that the border be the river. "A dry line will never do between us," they argued. "We may as well be annihilated at once, as to cede any portion of the land West of the river." Knowing that Georgia would accept nothing less, Adams warned the Indian delegates that they had better surrender all the lands claimed by the state if they expected to nullify the treaty. For weeks the two sides argued until, one by one, the Creeks' trusted advisers urged their delegation to abandon the Chattahoochee River boundary and give Georgia what it demanded. First Crowell, then the Indians' interpreter, William Hambly, and finally their Cherokee "secretaries" John Ridge and David Vann told them to sell. Frustrated and heartbroken by the prospective loss of Creek land, Opothle Yoholo was driven to attempt suicide.

On January 24, 1826, the Indian delegates finally deferred to the U.S. government and signed the Treaty of Washington. According to its terms, the Creeks would sell their lands claimed by Georgia, including a tract west of the Chattahoochee to be defined by a surveyor's line. In return they won the repudiation of the Treaty of Indian Springs, thereby saving their lands in Alabama. Moreover, the U.S. government promised to pay to the Creeks almost $250,000 for the cession plus $20,000 per year forever. The two sides also agreed on a plan by which the followers of William Mc-

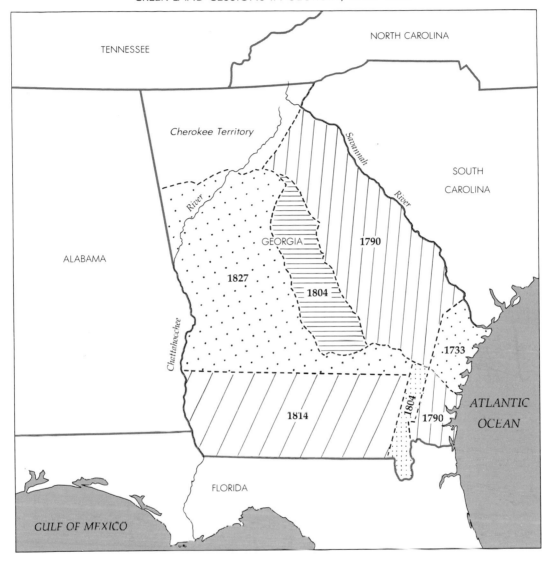

CREEK LAND CESSIONS IN GEORGIA, 1733–1827

Intosh could emigrate, or remove, to lands set aside for them west of the Mississippi River. Neither Georgia nor the Creeks were completely satisfied, but in a spirit of grudging compromise both groups agreed to the terms. On April 22, 1826, the U.S. Senate ratified the new treaty.

According to Secretary of State Henry Clay, the Treaty of Washington was "much more disadvantageous to the United States than the [Creeks]." Despite the Indians' land cession, they had won some important victories. For example, the United States recognized the right of the National Council to nullify the Treaty of Indian Springs. Never before and never again would the United States agree to tear up a treaty, regardless of how fraudulent or illegal. And as well as winning back their land in Alabama, the Creeks also received a guarantee from the United States that it would protect their right to live there free from harassment by non-Indians. Opothle Yoholo and the other delegates had tried their best to serve the interests of the Creek Nation, and under the circumstances they negotiated well.

During the several years after the ratification of the Treaty of Washington, many hundreds of Creeks took advantage of its provisions for removal to the West. The U.S. government surveyed and set aside land for them on the Arkansas River in what is now eastern Oklahoma, built an Indian agency, appointed David Brearley as Indian agent, and paid the costs of their move. At first, the emigrants were mostly the followers of William McIntosh from Coweta, but they were soon joined by other Lower Creeks. These Indians had to move out of the ceded lands in Georgia in any case, and some, fearing that they would be expelled from Alabama sooner or later, simply kept on going west. The National Council was glad to get rid of McIntosh's people, but as others began to follow, the headmen became worried. They knew that it would be increasingly difficult to hold on

to their Nation if their people were willing to remove. Every instance of Indian emigration encouraged the officials of Alabama and the United States to press harder for a cession of all the remaining Creek land. If emigration continued, many headmen believed there would not be enough Creeks in the East to justify their land claims to the federal government.

To prevent this voluntary emigration, the Council headmen introduced laws that made it illegal to move west. The Council sent lawmenders to break up the camps where migrants gathered and punished with public whippings any Creeks who tried to convince others to leave their southeastern homeland. Creek leaders preferred to persuade their people to remain in the Southeast by the logic of their argument, but they were also prepared to use force if necessary to keep the Nation whole. As a result, many Creeks came to resent the Council.

The Creeks' movement west was never large enough to completely justify the fears of the Council leaders, but it did cause problems for the Nation. The leaders were correct in believing that the emigrations weakened the Creeks' ability to resist those U.S. officials who argued that the entire tribe should be removed. The Alabama state legislature soon began to debate bills that would force the Creeks to be subject to state law. State leaders believed that by imposing harsh and foreign laws on the Creeks, the Indians' lives would become so miserable that they would all be eager to leave.

At the same time, Congress began to discuss a bill that called for the removal of all eastern Indian tribes to a western Indian Territory. In 1827, Secretary of War Peter Porter recommended that Congress enact legislation that would authorize negotiations with all the tribes living east of the Mississippi in which they would exchange their traditional homelands for new property in the West. Congress considered the proposal for some time but did not act on it. When Andrew Jackson became president in 1829, however, he threw his full weight behind the idea. He urged removal in his Inaugural Address and in his first State of the Union message, he orchestrated positive publicity for removal in the press, and his officials helped organize citizens' groups to write letters and sign petitions in support of the proposal.

Opponents of removal argued that the plan was an immoral violation of the letter and spirit of the treaties that the United States had signed with the Indian tribes. They replied to Jackson's lobbying with a publicity campaign of their own. The debate was "one of the severest struggles, that I have ever witnessed in Congress," wrote one congressman from Tennessee. When all was said and done, however, President Jackson had his way. On May 26, 1830, the Indian Removal Act passed the House of Representatives by the narrow margin of 102 to 97. The Senate approved it the next day, and Andrew Jackson signed the bill into law.

In its written form, the Indian Removal Act appeared quite innocent. It au-

President Andrew Jackson was the major force behind the Indian Removal Act of 1830. His policies caused many eastern Indian tribes to lose their homeland.

thorized the president to set aside land in the West for eastern tribes and to provide the Indians with title to that land. The bill also stipulated that the government would pay all members of the removed tribes for the homes and other properties they would have to leave behind, finance the costs of moving them plus their living expenses in the West for one year, and protect the people who removed from any "disturbance from any other tribe or nation of Indians, or from any other person or persons whatever." The U.S. Congress also stipulated that "nothing in th[e] act shall be construed as authorizing or directing the violation of any existing treaty between the United States and any of the Indian tribes." According to the terms and guarantees of the law, no tribe had to remove against its will. Only those tribes that voluntarily agreed in a treaty to exchange their eastern lands for new lands in the West could be removed.

The realities of the Indian Removal Act were quite different, however. Almost immediately after its passage, President Jackson appointed commissioners to negotiate removal treaties with eastern tribes. There were many Indian peoples in eastern North America, but most of the groups were small and had little land. The main targets for removal were the five largest and most powerful southeastern tribes—the Choctaws, the Chickasaws, the Seminoles, the Cherokees, and the Creeks. These tribes held rich cotton lands or, as in the case of the Cherokees, gold mines that were sought after by state officials and settlers. The tribes'

A 20th-century painting by Creek artist Jerome Tiger. The work depicts the hardships experienced by the Creeks during their 1835 removal to Indian Territory. The tribe may have lost some 40 percent of its population during the journey.

presence in the South also frightened slave owners, who feared that the abolitionist crusade against slavery would somehow be strengthened by the continued presence of large numbers of Indians, who were neither white nor slaves, in their states. North Carolina, Tennessee, Georgia, Alabama, Mississippi and Florida Territory still claimed Indian lands endorsed the Removal Act and demanded quick action from federal treaty commissioners. In order to speed up the process, Mississippi, and Tennessee joined Georgia and Alabama in extending their state laws over the Indians within their borders. They expected, correctly, that the Indians would find those laws so oppressive that removal would seem beneficial.

In 1830, the Choctaws of Mississippi became the first tribe to sign a removal treaty with the United States. The Seminoles of Florida signed one under duress in 1832, as did the Chickasaws of Tennessee and Mississippi. The people of these three tribes then made journeys to their new homeland in Indian Territory.

During this time, the Creeks negotiated a treaty with U.S. commissioners that was signed on March 24, 1832. However, it was not a removal treaty. The Creek delegation of seven headmen, led once again by Opothle Yoholo, was the fourth in three years appointed by the National Council to visit Washington. The committee had the same purpose as it had during previous trips—to protest the enforcement of Alabama law in the Nation and to appeal for the observance of the Indians' treaty rights. The Creeks particularly called for protection against non-Indian intruders who assumed that Alabama law gave them a blank check to enter the Nation, stake out claims, hunt, and otherwise harass the Creek people. But the Jackson administration approved of the actions of Alabama's legislature and citizens. Federal officials continually rebuffed the Creeks' complaints, telling them that if they did not like living under Alabama law, they should move west.

Tired of complaining without results, the fourth Creek delegation took the draft of a proposed treaty with them to Washington. The Council stated that "removal [is] the worst evil that can befall [us]" and proposed an arrangement that would permit their people to remain in Alabama. Their idea was to survey the Nation and divide it into square-mile sections that would be assigned to individual Creeks. Each head chief would receive five sections, each headman would get two, and each head of a family or adult without a family would get one. The Nation would set aside other sections for various special purposes, such as land for orphans. The Creeks would then sell all the unassigned sections. The chiefs' plan called for guarantees that all "our old customs and laws in relation to our local and internal affairs" would be protected and that Creeks in Alabama would have the same rights as did citizens of the state.

This proposal and requests for various pensions, compensations, and payments for land and improvements were presented by Opothle Yoholo to Secretary of

War Lewis Cass. He agreed to expel all the intruders living illegally in the Nation. But Cass insisted that the grants were too large and had to be reduced, to which the delegates agreed. The secretary also would not accept the guarantees requested by the Council. It would have to be left to the Alabama legislature to decide if the Creeks could enjoy equal citizenship rights or maintain their "old customs."

As the negotiations made clear, the Creeks obviously intended to stay in Alabama. They were willing to pay a high price to remain, however. By agreeing to accept individual sections of land, they were giving up their ancient principle of community land ownership. They intended to select tracts in blocks so they could continue their communal living patterns. But technically they were agreeing to dissolve the Creek Nation so that the Creek people could hold on to some of their homeland. The scheme depended on the goodwill of both the federal government and the state of Alabama, and the Creeks were taking an awful chance. Their only alternative, however, was to move west, and they were adamantly opposed to that. They had no choice but to have faith and hope for the best.

Unfortunately, the next four years offered the Creeks little hope. The federal government took only halfhearted steps to remove intruders, it was slow to survey the sections, and it was even slower in paying for the services and compensations stipulated in the treaty. Also, the Alabama legislature denied the Creeks full citizenship rights. Now, under Alabama law, the Indians could be arrested and sued in the courts, but they could not testify in their own defense. This situation opened the way to one of the biggest frauds in American history. Many Alabama whites claimed that Creeks owed them money, and the court confiscated the Indians' property as payment. Whites also robbed and beat Creeks without fear of arrest and often showed the courts fake deeds claiming that Creek people had sold them property. More often than not, the judges awarded the swindlers the lands of victimized Creeks.

In the spring of 1836, after four years of brutal harassment, a group of Creek men living near the Chattahoochee River attacked a number of Georgians who were coming to Alabama to join in the looting. Shortly thereafter, the warriors boarded and burned a steamboat as it made its way upriver to Columbus, Georgia, and then set fire to a bridge over the Chattahoochee River. This was all Alabama and the United States needed to justify an invasion of the Creek Nation. President Jackson ordered the army to round up all the Creek people and prepare them for forced removal west. In the name of national security, the United States would deport the Indians as quickly as possible and pay compensation for their lost homes, farms, livestock, and lands later. In violation of all the treaty provisions guaranteeing the Indians federal protection for their life and property, Jackson ordered that everyone had to go.

The removal of the Creek people took place during the final months of 1836 and

(continued on page 81)

FABRIC OF TRADITION

Creek women traditionally manufactured decorative clothing, bags, and other objects for everyday and ceremonial use. These items were woven or sewn using resources found in the Creeks' natural environment, such as animal skins and plant fibers.

In the 16th century, Europeans began to travel through Creek territory. These explorers brought with them fabrics and decorative techniques that were unknown to the native peoples of North America. The Creeks adapted these new items and ideas to their traditional technology. The result was a creative blend of Indian and European design.

For the most part, Creek women continued to make the same types of items they had in the past. However, they began to use European designs and materials, such as glass beads and wool and cotton fabric. The objects they created were as useful as they were beautiful.

Today, Creek women still make garments similar to those of their ancestors. Although this clothing is now worn only at ceremonies, it continues to proclaim the unique heritage of the Creeks.

Two sashes woven from strands of dyed wool, about 26 inches long. The Creeks usually wore sashes only on ceremonial occasions.

An early-18th-century pouch and belt woven on a loom from wool yarn. The edge of the flap is decorated with white glass trade beads. The item was owned by Creek leader and prophet Josiah Francis.

A mid-19th-century pouch and belt made from several pieces of dyed red strouding—a coarse wool manufactured by the British for trade with the Indians. The items are embellished with glass trade beads and yarn tassels.

Creek women made some types of clothing and other objects using a special technique known as finger weaving. By hand, finger weavers braided multiple strands of yarn, sometimes with beads attached, to create bands of fabric. They often left the ends unbraided to form tassels. The process was much cheaper and faster than weaving on a loom, but it also had limitations. Finger weavers could manage just a few strands of yarn at a time, so they could only produce garments that could be made from narrow fabric strips, such as sashes, garters, and other types of clothing.

A mid-20th-century man's sash that was worn during ceremonial games played between teams representing different Creek towns.

A ceremonial belt, approximately six feet long, made of yarn interwoven with white porcelain beads.

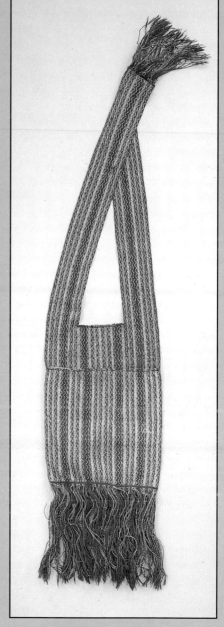

A late-18th-century pouch and belt made with European yarn and glass beads.

The breechcloth was one of the most common articles of clothing worn by Indian men and women. The garment, which consisted of a center piece and two flaps, was worn between the legs and held in place around the waist by folding the flaps over a belt.

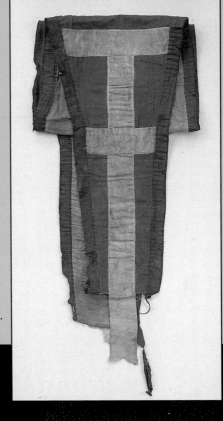

An early-20th-century cotton breechcloth.

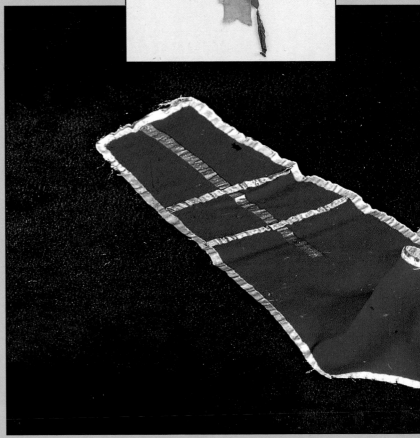

A flannel breechcloth from the 1890s, decorated with satin ribbon appliqué.

78

The four white crosses on this breechcloth, made in 1964, represent four allied Creek towns. The black central cross symbolizes the four corners of the world.

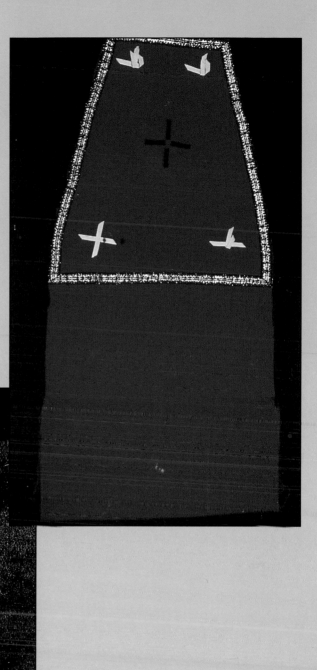

A Creek man's ceremonial sash, approximately 55 inches long, made in 1964 as part of his ceremonial game garb.

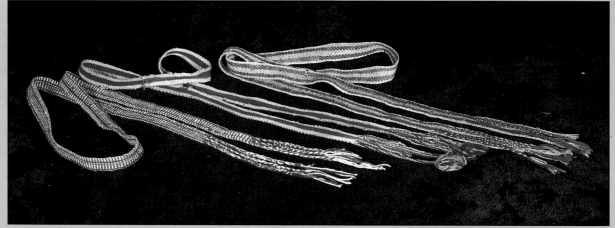

Three early-20th-century fringed sashes.

(continued from page 72)

the spring and summer of 1837. In groups ranging in size from several hundred to more than 2,000, U.S. Army troops herded the Creeks west. Some of the old and very young rode in wagons, but most walked. Conditions were horrible. As one observer wrote from Little Rock, Arkansas, in December 1836:

> Thousands of them are entirely destitute of shoes or cover of any kind for their feet; many of them are almost naked, and but few of them [have] anything more on their persons than a light dress calculated only for the summer, or for a warm climate. In this destitute condition, they are wading in cold mud, or are hurried on over the frozen ground, as the case may be. Many of them have in this way had their feet frost-bitten; and being unable to travel, fall in the rear of the main party, and in this way are left on the road to await the ability or convenience of the contractors to assist them. Many of them, not being able to endure this

A Creek chief (center) and his family as drawn in the 1830s by the American artist George Catlin (1796–1872). Catlin spent much of his life recording the Indian cultures of North America.

REMOVAL ROUTES OF THE CREEKS

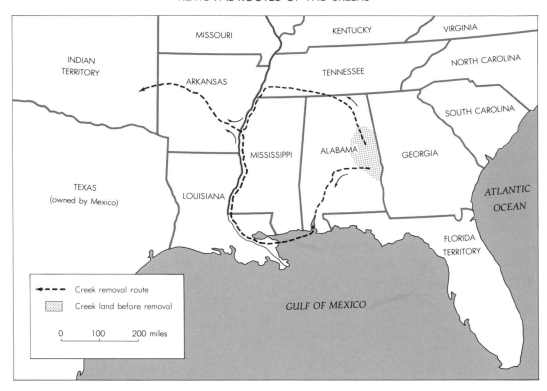

unexampled state of human suffering, die, and are thrown by the side of the road, and are covered over only with brush, etc.—where they remain until devoured by the wolves.

It is now past the middle of December, and the winter, though cold, is by no means at its worst stage, and when the extreme of winter does fall upon these most miserable creatures, in their present suffering and desperate condition, the destruction of human life will be most deplorable.

Some Creeks were taken by a southern route to New Orleans and then brought on steamboats up the Mississippi River to Arkansas. But, as an observer noted, the contractors responsible for organizing the removal chartered

rotten, old, and unseaworthy boats, because they were of a class to be procured cheaply; and then to make those increased profits still larger, the Indians were packed upon these crazy vessels in such crowds, that not the slightest regard seems to have been paid to their safety, comfort, or even decency. The crammed condition of the decks and cabins was offensive to every sense and feeling, and kept the poor creatures in a state unfit for human beings.

One of these boats, the *Monmouth*, was being piloted up the wrong side of the river by a drunken crew and collided with another boat, the *Trenton*. There were more than 600 Creeks on the *Monmouth*, and when the boat broke up and sank, more than 300 of them drowned. Many of the survivors were badly scalded by steam after the boat's boilers burst.

No one has ever compiled a complete list of the Creeks who died while being "drove off like dogs," according to a Creek man from Cusseta. Scholars often guess that the death toll was 3,500. The total population on the eve of removal was probably more than 25,000, but a census made by the Bureau of Indian Affairs (BIA) in 1857 in Oklahoma counted only 14,888. In a 25-year period, the Creeks lost some 40 percent of their people.

A few Creeks remained in Alabama in a community along Poarch Creek. They were descended from only about a dozen mixed-blood Creeks who held on to reservations granted to them in the Treaty of Fort Jackson. But these people were surrounded by non-Indians and, with so many of their relatives and neighbors gone, soon adopted many mainstream American practices. By the mid-1800s, the traditional Creek Nation in the East ceased to exist. ▲

A 1900 photograph of Granny Spot, one of the many Creeks who re-moved to Indian Territory.

THE
CREEK NATION
IN THE WEST

When the last remnants of the eastern Creeks arrived in Indian Territory in 1837, they found that the followers of William McIntosh and others (numbering about 3,000) who had moved to Indian Territory during the preceding 10 years had already reestablished there many aspects of Creek traditional culture. Not all of them were Lower Creeks from Coweta, the home of McIntosh, but there were enough of them to keep his half brother, Roley McIntosh, in power as their leader. Other Lower Creeks had also come west, as did a few Upper Creeks, such as the Baptist preacher John Davis from Tuckabatchee. They, too, had fallen into line behind the McIntosh family.

The settlers fought hard to survive. They erected new homes, transplanted their religious and political institutions, and worked hard to strengthen their small but independent Indian republic. The transplanted Creeks built new towns and farms on the Arkansas and Verdigris rivers near the U.S Army outpost Fort Gibson. Staying close to the rivers, they planted cornfields and attempted to replicate as much as they could the life they left behind in the East. Under Roley McIntosh's leadership, the Creeks in the West soon began to prosper.

The Creeks in the West were as influenced by mainstream American culture as they had been in the East. Often slave owners, they grew corn, cotton, and other crops for sale at the markets in Fort Gibson and Fort Smith in Arkansas and in New Orleans. Many were motivated by a desire for profits, which they spent on consumer goods. In a variety of ways, the western Creeks displayed a style of life that more resembled that of prosper-

85

ous southern non-Indian farmers than that of traditional Creeks.

The social, economic, and political stability of the newly established western Creek Nation was presented a major challenge when the majority of the eastern Creeks migrated to Indian Territory in 1836–37. The western Creeks had spent a decade putting their life in Indian Territory in order and were not at all happy about the prospect of hosting some 16,000 newcomers. Indeed, most of the western Creeks looked on the new arrivals as uncultured traditionalists.

The easterners, led by Opothle Yoholo, began to arrive at Fort Gibson in December 1836. It was terribly cold, snowy, and icy, and the travelers were suffering badly after their long and stressful journey. The troops at Fort Gibson were on the alert because they feared trouble between the two groups of Creeks. But Roley McIntosh and Opothle Yoholo avoided conflicts by making an arrangement by which the newcomers would settle on the southwestern portion of the Creeks' reserved lands and build their towns along the Canadian River and its tributaries. However, many of the newcomers already had friends and relatives among the western Creeks and settled in their midst instead. As a result, the two groups ended up having nearly equal populations. Although the Lower Creeks lived predominantly in the Arkansas Valley and the Upper Creeks in the Canadian Valley, the two groups intermixed enough so that Upper and Lower distinctions no longer made much sense.

The groups soon became known simply as the Arkansas Creeks and the Canadian Creeks. Between the 2 clusters of settlements were about 50 miles of prairie, which for several years remained largely unsettled.

The Canadian and Arkansas Creeks adjusted to their new homeland in different ways. The Canadian Creeks tended to live in traditional towns, raise their crops in large communal fields (one cornfield on the Canadian River measured 3 by 8 miles), and maintain their traditional ceremonial life and manner of dress. Perhaps most important, the Canadian Creeks perpetuated their traditional economic system, in which the town leaders took charge of the harvest and the tribe's annuity payments. The headmen then distributed the crops to families according to their needs and used the annuity money for public works projects, including gristmills and ferries. This system both assured equal access to the necessities of life and kept strong the traditional system of town government. It also preserved the ethic of generosity and sharing, the most highly esteemed personal virtue of traditional Creek culture.

On the other hand, the Creeks on the Arkansas River continued to look to Anglo-American culture for guidance. In the words of the Creek agent James Logan, they "manifested a strong desire to throw off all their old superstitious ways and customs and to adopt the ways of the whites." These Indians most often lived in the Arkansas and Verdigris valleys on independent family farmsteads, wore the same clothes as non-Indian farmers, and used slaves. They were relatively uninterested in maintaining the old style of town life. During the summer of 1845, for example, serious floods destroyed the crops and farms of many Creeks living in the Verdigris Valley. Creeks on the Arkansas were not so badly hit and produced their normal harvest. But they would not share their bounty with the farmers who lost their crops. As Agent James Logan wrote: "This [surplus] is in the hands of individuals not generally disposed to acts of charity, or to alleviating the distress of their suffering brethren, and would not be willing to part with [their surplus corn] without its just equivalent in money, which the poor sufferers generally have not." Logan also failed to convince the headmen of the Arkansas Creeks to part with some of the annuity money for the benefit of the flood victims. If such a disaster had occurred among the Canadian Creeks, the traditional system of redistributing resources would have taken care of those in need.

The inhabitants of the Arkansas Creek settlements were also more open to Christianity and non-Indian education. Many of the original settlers in the Arkansas Valley had converted to Christianity in the East, and some, like John Davis, had attended school and become preachers in Indian Territory. By the time the main migration of eastern exiles occurred, Presbyterian, Baptist, and Methodist congregations had already formed in the Arkansas Valley settlements. In or-

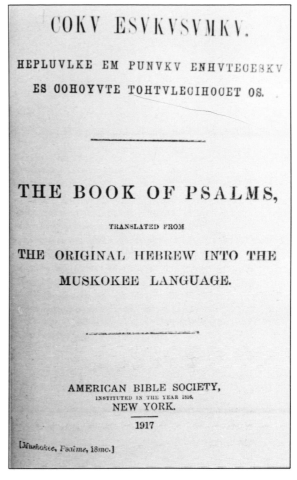

The title page of a Bible written in Muskogee, the language spoken by most Creeks.

der to further promote Christianity among the Creeks, Presbyterian missionary John Fleming created a written alphabet of the Muskogee language with the help of James Perryman, a well-educated Arkansas Creek Christian. In 1835 they published *Istutsi In Naktsoka*, a children's reader, and during the next few years produced a hymnal, portions of the Bible, and several other readers in Muskogee.

The newcomers, however, opposed the religious and educational practices of non-Indians. Indeed, Opothle Yoholo had called for the expulsion of white preachers from the Nation as part of the arrangement he made with Roley McIntosh in December 1836. He also rec-

The Tullahassee Mission, which was founded on the Creek reservation in 1850 by Presbyterian missionary Robert M. Loughridge. The mission was one of several institutions designed to teach Creek children non-Indian practices and values.

ommended that any Creek who preached Christianity or attended church be punished with a public whipping of from 50 to 100 lashes. The Arkansas River Creeks agreed with the terms because they were afraid that the missionaries might preach resistance to the Indians' slaves. They were also concerned because of a scandal in which a married Creek woman apparently became involved with a Methodist missionary.

However, many of the non-Christian Creeks soon came to oppose the ban because the missionaries were the only schoolteachers in the Nation. Creek parents wanted to make sure that their children learned how to deal successfully with English-speaking white people. Their protests were effective, and in 1841 the Council negotiated a contract with the Presbyterian church. According to the document, the Presbyterians would construct a boarding school on the Creek reservation and provide missionaries to teach there. In 1843, the Reverend Robert M. Loughridge, who later prepared and published a Muskogee-English dictionary, opened a school at Coweta (the Creeks named all their new towns after those in the East) among the Arkansas Creeks.

Soon Roley McIntosh and other Arkansas Valley leaders began to urge that the ban on preaching be lifted, and in 1848 the Council ended its prohibition of Christianity. By that time, the Presbyterians had opened another boarding school in the Arkansas settlement of Tullahassee, and the Methodists had established the Asbury School at North Fork Town among the Canadian Creeks. But classes at these schools were conducted in English, making it very difficult for students to succeed unless they could already speak English. And because there were few English-speaking families in the Canadian settlements, few children from that part of the Nation attended school. This situation only increased the cultural gulf between the Canadian and Arkansas settlements. Traditional values remained strong among the Canadian Creeks, but mainstream American culture grew stronger among the Arkansas Creeks.

Government became the one unifying factor in the new Creek Nation. Under the terms of the 1836 agreement, the Arkansas and Canadian settlements had governed themselves according to their own values and in their own separate councils. But in 1840 they decided to reestablish the National Council. At the halfway point between the two settlements, the Creeks built a large council house in a grove where there was a good spring. There the Council met once a year. As in the East, each of the two groups of settlements selected its own principal chief. Under their guidance, the headmen from the various towns conducted national business. Roley McIntosh was principal chief of the Arkansas Creeks and remained in office for many years. The Canadian Creeks, on the other hand, chose several principal chiefs. Although Opothle Yoholo was rarely their official leader, he remained the most influential figure among them.

The newly established western Creek government, which perpetuated the district councils as well as the National Council, continued in operation until 1859 or 1860. At that time, the Council prepared a written constitution that provided for the election of officers and the establishment of a court system and electoral districts. The new constitutional system did not go into effect, however. Its institution was interrupted when growing tensions between Northern and Southern states in the East erupted into the Civil War.

The Creeks in Indian Territory were well aware of these tensions. All the Indian agents among them were Southerners, and beginning in 1859 or 1860 these officials kept the Indians informed of the Southern interpretation of the growing conflict. For example, popular and successful Creek agent William H. Garrett, who was appointed in 1853, was a citizen of South Carolina, a proslavery state. His views coincided with the interests of many Creeks. Some 10 or 15 percent of the inhabitants of the Creek Nation were black, most of whom were slaves. Creek slave owners tended to look to the non-Indian plantation owners of the South for role models, and therefore many of them naturally sympathized with the Southern, or Confederate, states. Many Creeks also had economic or social connections with the neighboring Confederate state of Arkansas, and some had attended college there. Therefore, when the Southern states declared their independence from the United States, or seceded, during the winter of 1860–61, many of the Creeks sided with the Confederate States of America.

The Confederacy encouraged Creek support because it hoped to gain control of Indian Territory as a buffer between the Northern states, or Union, and pro-slavery Texas. In the spring of 1861, the Confederate Congress sent Albert Pike of Arkansas into Indian Territory to negotiate treaties of alliance with the major Indian groups, known as the Five Tribes—the Chickasaws, the Choctaws, the Seminoles, the Cherokees, and the Creeks. Pike met with the Creeks at North Fork Town and presented them with a treaty of alliance. Several Canadian Creek leaders, including Opothle Yoholo and Oktarharsars Harjo (also called Sands), opposed Pike's proposal. But enough Creek headmen, including Moty Kennard, Echo Harjo, Chilly McIntosh, and Daniel N. McIntosh, approved and signed the treaty to make it binding. The document, dated July 10, 1861, was the first of five treaties signed by Indian Territory tribes and the Confederacy.

The Canadian Creeks opposed the treaty not because they supported the Union but because they did not believe it was the best course of action for the Nation. Indeed, Opothle Yoholo was one of the largest slaveholders in the Creek Nation and thus no abolitionist. He believed the Creeks should remain neutral in what he saw as a white man's war. Other leaders, such as Cherokee Principal Chief John Ross, also opposed involvement in the Civil War but agreed to follow the

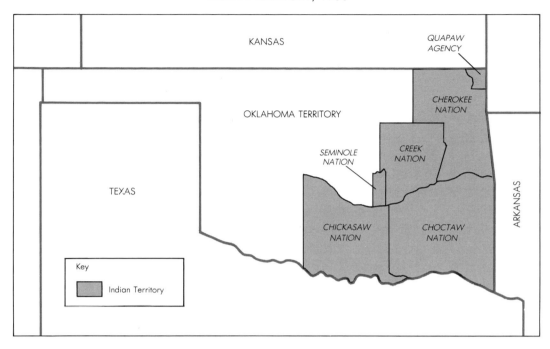

decisions of their people if they chose to take sides. Opothle Yoholo, however, refused to back down. Instead, he gathered on his plantation near North Fork Town all the Creeks who opposed an alliance with the Confederacy. The group ultimately included about half the people of the Nation, the majority of whom were traditional Creeks from the Canadian district, their slaves, and the escaped slaves of Confederate Creeks, who had been treated badly by their owners. Once again the Creek Nation was divided between the traditionalists and the Anglo-American-influenced Indians.

After the Confederate treaty was approved, Agent Garrett began to organize Creek volunteers for service in the Con-

federate army. Daniel N. McIntosh received a commission as colonel in command of a regiment, and his half brother Chilly was appointed lieutenant colonel in command of a battalion. Colonel Douglas H. Cooper, a Texan who previously had been federal agent among the Choctaw, assumed command of all the troops in Indian Territory, which included perhaps 1,375 soldiers.

The growing number of supporters at Opothle Yoholo's plantation worried the Confederate Creeks. And the growing number of Confederate troops in Indian Territory, including cavalry from Arkansas and Texas, worried the neutrals. In November 1861, Opothle Yoholo decided to lead his followers north into Kansas to

Canadian River Creek leader Oktarharsars Harjo (also known as Sands) headed the Loyal Creek faction. In 1867, he and his followers vehemently opposed the creation of a constitutional government for the Creek Nation.

seek the protection of Union troops. Major George A. Catlin had assured Opothle Yoholo in a letter that the U.S. government would shelter there and care for all the Creeks who opposed the Confederate treaty. Toward the onset of winter, Opothle Yoholo, who was an old man (perhaps 80), left for Kansas leading a group of several thousand people. They brought with them as many of their possessions as they could carry in hundreds of farm wagons and buggies, as well as several thousand head of cattle and horses.

Colonel Cooper and his Confederate Creek troops pursued them. Between the middle of November and the end of December the opposing forces engaged in three battles. These conflicts, as well as the confusion of the long trek and bad weather, caused the refugees to lose all of their livestock and most of their belongings. Many stumbled into Kansas on foot, starving, exhausted, and freezing with cold. Soon there were nearly 6,000 escapees for the federal government to house and feed. The agent, unprepared for so many who were in such desperate need, housed them in tents. Not long after, Opothle Yoholo died from exposure.

The warfare quickly devastated eastern Indian Territory, including much of the Creek Nation. During the fighting, invading soldiers and looters burned the Creeks' towns and farms, killed their livestock, and destroyed their fields. Most of the civilian relatives of the Confederate Creeks escaped the battles by fleeing south into the Choctaw Nation or Texas, but their lot as war refugees was not much better than that of Opothle Yoholo's followers in Kansas. By the time the war was over and the people returned, there was virtually nothing left to salvage but the land.

On April 9, 1865, the U.S. Civil War ended when Confederate army general Robert E. Lee officially surrendered to Union army general Ulysses S. Grant. In the fall of 1865, federal officials requested that delegations from the Five Tribes be sent to Fort Smith to negotiate new treaties with the United States. For the Creeks, there were two overriding issues: the reunification of their nation and the reestablishment of relations with the United States. Neither problem could be resolved without the agreement of both factions of Creeks. Therefore, both sides sent representatives. Sands led the so-called neutral group, many of whom had actually fought in the Union army and by the end of the war considered themselves Loyal, or Unionist, Creeks. For this reason, the Loyalists reasonably believed they deserved recognition from the U.S. government for their contributions to the war effort, as well as compensation for their losses. They also assumed that they would be encouraged by the United States to take up the reins of Creek national government.

On the other hand, Daniel McIntosh and the Confederate Creeks saw themselves as the most likely group to control the new Creek government. They believed they were more intelligent, better educated, more "civilized," and more reasonable than the Loyalists. As Confederate Creek regiment veteran George W. Grayson stated, "The Southern Creeks could not brook the idea of being dominated and governed by the ignorance of the northern Indians supplemented by that of their late negro slaves." And, according to Grayson, the federal government sympathized with the prejudices of the Southern faction.

The authorities at Washington recognized clearly that the Southern Creeks had a clear understanding of the restored relation between the Creek nation as a unit and the United States. [Indeed, the federal

George W. Grayson was a member of the Confederate Creek regiment during the Civil War and a staunch supporter of the constitutional government.

government] upheld the policy and contentions in the main of the Southern Creeks and the more intelligent of the Northern element who now were in sympathy with the policy advocated by the Southern Creeks.

At the Fort Smith Peace Conference, the U.S. representatives chose to ignore the contributions of the pro-Union Creek faction and insisted on treating all the

Indians as conquered enemies. The federal commissioners told the Creeks that they would have to travel to Washington and sign new treaties with the United States. Their treaty with the Confederate States of America had voided all their previous treaties with the U.S. government. In order to reestablish their ties with the United States, the Creeks would have to be prepared to sell the western half of their nation, free and make full citizens of all their slaves, agree to allows railroads to be constructed through their country, and accept a territorial government under Congressional control.

In January 1866, delegates representing the two Creek factions arrived in Washington. The Loyalists, represented by Sands, Coweta Mico, and Cotchochee, were browbeaten by the federal negotiators into accepting the demands of the U.S. government. However, the Confederate Creek delegates Daniel McIntosh and James M. C. Smith protested several provisions of the treaty. They told the negotiators that 30 cents per acre was too low a price for the Creeks' nearly 4-million-acre land cession, and they argued that $775,000 was too large an amount to be set aside from the sale for compensating the Loyal Creeks. On June 14, 1866, after agreeing to reduce the compensation sum to $100,000, the two sets of delegates came to an understanding and signed the treaty.

Throughout 1867, leaders of the Northern and Southern factions worked on the problem of reuniting the nation. After months of consultation, they created a committee made up of representatives from both factions. The group drew up a national constitution and a code of civil and criminal law. In accordance with the new constitution, the Creeks created a legislature, which they called the National Council, that consisted of two houses—the House of Kings and the House of Warriors. The leaders of the individual Creek towns chose council members according to the traditional system of representation. The new Creek government was presided over by an executive branch—a principal and second chief—elected by popular vote of adult male citizens, including freed blacks and intermarried white men. The Council was responsible for appointing the national treasurer and the national interpreter. The Creeks also created a judicial branch that encompassed a court system divided into six districts and a Supreme Court composed of five justices. These courts enforced the new legal code, which was mainly an adaptation of the prewar system.

The first election day in the Creek Nation was the first Monday of November 1867. When the voting was over, Samuel Checote, a Methodist minister and former officer in the Confederate Creek regiment, had been elected principal chief of the Creek Nation. He defeated the Loyal Creek candidate, Sands, whose followers reportedly did not understand how to cast their vote.

The new constitutional government went a long way toward healing the breach between Loyal and Confederate Creeks, but it created a new factional conflict that would dominate Creek politics for the next 50 years. The Creek Nation had experienced internal conflicts since the beginning of its recorded history, but the characteristics of the groups continually changed. There was no straight line that led from one faction to the next in the various issues that

Samuel Checote, principal chief of the Creek Nation, was a Methodist minister and Confederate veteran.

divided the Nation. For example, in the 1820s the Creeks had formed two groups—one that supported William McIntosh and one that supported Opothle Yoholo. Because the McIntosh family led the Confederates and Opothle Yoholo headed the neutral Creeks, some scholars have wrongly surmised that the Civil War division was a simple continuation of an earlier conflict. And because Samuel Checote was aligned with the Confederate Creeks and Sands with the Loyalists, scholars have also wrongly believed that this division merely perpetuated previous factional disputes. In reality, Creek politics was a complicated system of shifting alignments just like that of the United States.

The newest dispute in the Creek Nation was between those who supported the new constitutional government and those who opposed it. The Creek people had for hundreds of years been governed by a system of town and regional councils. They had only reluctantly and under great pressure formed the National Council in the early 18th century. A large number of Creeks were opposed to any further tampering with their method of government. Many believed that the old National Council system could still provide the Creeks with adequate governance and opposed the new constitution, to which Sands referred as "the same as the white man's law." Most of the people who felt this way lived in traditional towns, still practiced traditional ways, and contin-

ued to embrace traditional Creek culture. Most had not attended the mission schools, were not Christians, and probably did not speak English. These Creek people were the ones whom Confederate Creek George Grayson had called "ignorant." They are also the Creeks that scholars often refer to as full-bloods, an unfortunate term because the Indians' opinions were based on tradition and culture rather than genetics.

Much of the conflict was based on self-interest, as well. Principal Chief Checote, the McIntoshes, and other Confederate Creeks had bitterly opposed granting the freed slaves citizenship because they would likely vote against Confederates in Creek elections. Checote led a campaign to prohibit intermarriage between blacks and Creeks. For this reason, perhaps, the black inhabitants of the Nation aligned with the traditional Creeks in opposing the constitution.

Sands and his followers became increasingly vocal after the Civil War in their disaffection with the constitutional government. More and more of the Creek people denounced the new government, disclaimed its laws, and declared that they would not be bound by its decisions. The unrest came to a head in October 1871 when Sands and about 300 armed followers broke up the annual session of the National Council. Chief Checote called in the Creek militia to quell the "rebellion," which lasted for several days. The tense situation quieted for a time when Sands died the next year.

In 1875, however, the conflict heated up again when Chief Checote, having already served two terms, lost to Lochar Harjo, a prominent supporter of Sands. But because Checote's followers controlled the National Council, they impeached Lochar Harjo in 1876 and elevated Second Chief Ward Coachman, one of their fellow Confederate Creeks, into the vacated office. This action inflamed the traditionalists, as did Checote's reelection in 1879 to a third term as principal chief. Shortly thereafter Checote again enraged the Sands supporters by ordering the removal of Isparhechar, the justice of the Okmulgee District Court, after he was charged with misuse of his official power. Isparhechar had always been a staunch member of the proconstitution faction, but joined Sands's followers in his fury over being unseated. He then led them in a campaign to establish a new National Council under the traditional Creek system.

In 1881, Creek police broke up a meeting of Isparhechar's followers and arrested Heneha Chopco. Some of Heneha Chopco's friends came to his rescue and killed the law officers. The conflict became known as the Green Peach War because it broke out in a grove of unripened peaches. In retaliation, Chief Checote called on Pleasant Porter, a Confederate Creek regiment veteran and commanding officer of the Creek militia, to apprehend the mur-

Lochar Harjo, a supporter of Sands, was elected in 1875 to the office of principal chief. In a controversial episode, Creek council members loyal to Samuel Checote impeached Lochar Harjo and replaced him with one of their own supporters.

The residence of Pleasant Porter, commanding officer of the Creek militia during the Green Peach War and principal chief of the Creek Nation during the early 1900s.

derers. Porter and his militia chased Isparhechar and several hundred followers onto the Kiowa reservation, where federal troops captured them and transported them to Fort Gibson in 1883. The group was then reprimanded and released after a conciliatory meeting with Checote. The traditionalist faction had lost at every turn.

The conflict among the Creeks concerning their constitutional government was real enough, but the tribe would soon have to face a more formidable enemy. The Creek Nation was being, quite literally, invaded. It was not a military invasion, however. If anything, it was more dangerous. The invaders were stockmen and ranchers who drove their cattle through the Nation to market with increasing frequency, construction gangs laying down new railroad lines through Indian Territory, and white intruders, both crooked and honest, who in the late-1800s began to flock into the Nation in defiance of U.S. treaties with the Creeks. The federal government encouraged this invasion as the first step in an emerging policy to destroy Indian communities and force their inhabitants to enter the dominant Anglo-American society. ▲

The members of the Dawes Commission and a delegation of Creeks photographed in Washington, D.C., in 1899. The Creek group included such leaders as Isparhechar (seated, third from right), Roley McIntosh (seated, second from right), and George Grayson (last row, third from left).

ALLOTMENT
AND
REVITALIZATION

During the 1880s, a new group of reformers gained control of federal Indian policy. These people, who thought of themselves as humanitarians, were searching for a way to force Indians to conform to the cultural values of Anglo-Americans. Most believed that the quickest way to achieve this was to force them to abandon their communities, their common ownership of land, their systems of tribal governments, their religions, and indeed everything about them that kept them distinct from Anglo-Americans.

Missionaries and others had been trying for generations to change the cultures of Indians by introducing non-Indian farming techniques, religions, tools, and languages to tribes. Although these attempts had brought about a few changes, many tribes still maintained an identity separate from that of non-Indian Americans. The most prominent aspect of the Indians' separateness was their tribal organization, which was most visible in their system of communal landholding. The reformers believed that the easiest way to destroy the Creeks' way of life was to break up that system. Therefore, it became the main target of the reformers.

Federal Indian policymakers had been arguing since Thomas Jefferson's presidency that the only way to "civilize" the Indians was to provide them with individual plots of land, thus instilling in them the American ideal of private ownership. Indian resistance prevented this from happening, so reformers had to use other methods, such as non-Indian religions and education, to bring about the desired culture change. Most Indians rejected these actions as well. But as evi-

A Creek family outside their home in Indian Territory, photographed in the 1880s. The woman is pounding corn into meal.

dence began to surface of corruption in the Indian office and suffering on the reservation, the majority of Americans called for reform. Crusaders stepped up efforts to break up the Indians' communities, and this time Congress and the public ignored the Indians' protests. Senator Henry L. Dawes of Massachusetts sponsored a bill that proposed dividing communal Indian lands into small parcels, or allotments, and giving them to individual tribespeople. Dawes's bill also eradicated tribal governments and opened up surplus reservation land to white settlement.

In 1887, Congress passed this legislation in the General Allotment Act, or Dawes Act, and proclaimed that it contained the "final solution to the Indian Problem." However, the act expressly exempted from its provisions the tribes in Indian Territory, including the Creeks. But neither Congress nor the reformers ever intended that these tribes would escape allotment. In 1893, Congress created a special commission, headed by Senator Dawes, to negotiate allotment agreements specifically with the Five Tribes.

The threat of allotment horrified the Creeks. As Confederate Creek veteran George Grayson wrote, they were "paralyzed for a time [by] its bold effrontery." The Indians soon realized that they would have to face the issue and in 1895 elected Isparhechar, the "rebel" who had tried in the early 1880s to create a traditional government, as principal chief. In 1897 the Creek National Council sent a delegation to Muskogee to talk with the Dawes Commission. The Creek representatives deliberated over the terms of the treaty and rejected the commission's proposals, as did the representatives of the Choctaws, Chickasaws, Seminoles, and Cherokees.

To crush the Indians' resistance, Congress passed the Curtis Act in 1898. The legislation mandated allotment, abolished the tribal court system, and required that all laws passed by tribal governments be approved by the president of the United States. In the meantime, the Creek National Council prepared to fight allotment in the courts.

The Indians planned to sue the U.S. government, charging that the Curtis Act violated the terms of the Treaty of 1866, but President William McKinley vetoed the council's appropriation of funds to finance the suit.

Prinicipal Chief Pleasant Porter (left) and Isparhechar, a traditionalist leader, photographed in 1900.

The majority of the Creek people submitted to the Dawes Commission's demands, but they had a variety of reasons for doing so. Some had been educated in the Creek or missionary school systems or were associated in some way with the non-Indian economy. Others had connections with the federal government or somehow became convinced that allotment was inevitable. No matter what the reason, these tribe members became part of the official Creek Nation roll compiled by the federal commissioners. Those who enrolled selected allotments and received certificates that served as titles to them. Forced to deal with the Dawes Commis-

Chitto Harjo (Crazy Snake) and his followers, photographed in 1901. Crazy Snake is standing at the far right.

sion, the Creek National Council concentrated on negotiating the best deal possible for the Creek people. Despite their efforts, many tribe members either remained uninformed or adamantly refused to accept or cooperate with the allotment process. Others were never found despite the best efforts of the National Council to seek them out.

Although many Creeks rejected the terms proposed by the Dawes Commission from the outset, they did not organize a resistance movement until the winter of 1900–1901. At that time, a group of well-informed Creeks organized to campaign against enrollment and allotment. Their spokesperson, Chitto Harjo, was widely believed to have been their leader, as well. His name was a Snake clan war title that meant "recklessly brave snake," but the American press and local whites referred to him as Crazy Snake. Consequently, they called his followers and any other Creeks who opposed allotment Snake Indians.

In reaction to the Dawes Commission, Chitto Harjo and the so-called Snake Indians established a traditional Creek government at Hickory Ground, a Creek town on the north fork of the Canadian River. The Creeks who gathered there set up a National Council that passed laws prohibiting allotment, forbidding Creeks from hiring whites to work for them or encouraging whites to move into the Nation and threatening to punish violators with 50 lashes. The council published the laws and posted them throughout the Nation. It also appointed lawmenders to enforce them. The Snake Indians cited the Creek Nation's previous treaties with the United States, especially the treaty of 1832, which had guaranteed them self-government, as grounds for opposing allotment. By creating a separate government, they were also dissociating themselves from the Creeks' constitutional government that negotiated with the Dawes Commission.

Pleasant Porter, the recognized principal chief of the Nation, saw the Snake Indian movement as just another effort by traditional Creeks to undermine his power. He called on federal officials to help him stop them from threatening his position and the efforts of the allotment supporters. In the spring of 1901, U.S. marshals and troops raided Hickory Ground, broke up the "rebel" government, and arrested and jailed some 100 traditional Creek people. Tried before Judge John R. Thomas of the U.S. District Court at Muskogee, the Snake Indians were found guilty and sentenced to harsh prison terms. Judge Thomas then offered to suspend the convictions if the Indians promised to accept their allotments. But most did not, despite their promises, and in the end the Dawes Commission assigned allotments to only 1,331 Creek people—about 10 percent of the total number of Creeks entitled to them.

The Snake Indians gave up their opposition government, but Chitto Harjo remained an eloquent spokesperson for those who continued to resist allotment. He and other Snakes traveled to Washington several times to argue their position before Congress. At a special senatorial hearing conducted in 1906 in

Tulsa, Oklahoma, Chitto Harjo was a star witness. In a long and detailed recounting of the relations between the Creeks and the United States, Chitto Harjo cited provisions of treaties that guaranteed Creek self-government and argued that the Indians had done nothing to justify or legalize the United States's nullification of those treaty guarantees. But Chitto Harjo's eloquence came too late. Congress was in no mood to reverse its allotment policy. Indeed, Congress had already passed a law providing for Indian Territory and Oklahoma Territory to be admitted into the Union as the state of Oklahoma.

The territorial officials of Oklahoma had several obstacles to overcome in their quest for statehood. In 1866, the United States had taken the western half of Indian Territory from the Five Tribes in the Civil War treaties. The federal government intended to convert that land into reservations for several of the Great Plains tribes, including the Kiowas and the Comanches. After the reservations were assigned, an unclaimed tract of 2 million acres in the center of Indian Territory remained, and in 1889 the United States opened this region for settlement by whites. The next year, Congress organized the area as Oklahoma Territory. During the next several years, the government allotted the Plains Indians' reservations and made the "surplus" reservation land available for non-Indian settlement. Congress then extended the boundaries of Oklahoma Territory to include all of the western half of Indian Territory. By 1900, the present state of

Oklahoma was split nearly in half—the western part organized as Oklahoma Territory, the eastern part remaining as Indian Territory. The white settlers of Oklahoma Territory were eager for statehood and wanted the rest of the Indians' land to be incorporated into the new state. Of course, the Indian leaders of Indian Territory strongly opposed the prospect of their region being swallowed up by a state dominated by whites.

The Five Tribes decided that the best way to fight annihilation was to seek admission to the Union as a separate Indian state. After some preliminary discussions by each of the tribal governments, the principal chiefs of all but the Chickasaws issued a call for a constitutional convention to meet in August 1905 at Muskogee. Chief Porter of the Creeks was elected to preside over the convention "of delegates, [the list of which]," according to historian Angie Debo, "reads like a roll call of the great names in recent tribal history." The convention drafted a constitution for the new state, Sequoyah, a name suggested by Creek poet and journalist Alexander Posey in honor of the Cherokee Indian who had invented a syllabary for the Cherokee language some 80 years before. The Five Tribes submitted the constitution to their citizens in November, and although the turnout was light, the vote was overwhelmingly in its favor. The tribal leaders then submitted their proposal and constitution to the U.S. federal government, but Congress chose to ignore it. It instead ordered that the two territories be joined together to form the state of Oklahoma, in which In-

Creek Indians traveling to Muskogee, Oklahoma, to vote in the 1903 election for principal chief.

dians would be a minority. When Oklahoma entered the Union in October 1907, Indian Territory, along with the five Indian republics, ceased to exist.

The Creeks continued to live reasonably well on their allotments during the early 20th century but their situation soon worsened. At first, the majority of Creeks lived on compact 160-acre parcels. These homesteads were located mainly in the river valleys where the first Creek immigrants to the West had originally set

(continued on page 110)

THE DEVIL'S SHOESTRING

The Creek Indians have always lived near water. In fact, their name is a shortened version of Ochese Creek, one of the tributaries along which they traditionally built their villages. Because they lived so close to the water, the Creeks naturally took advantage of its main food resource—fish. They used many tools to catch them, including nets, hooks, and damlike weirs.

The most unusual fishing technique employed by the Creeks involved an herb known as the devil's shoestring. Creek men would pound the leaves of this plant into a powder, sprinkle it into a still body of water, and wade around in the pool to mix in the powder. Although harmless to humans, devil's shoestring was poisonous to fish. When the stunned fish floated to the surface, the fishermen could simply gather them up. This fishing method provided the Creeks with a large and easily acquired amount of food.

In 1835, the Creeks were relocated by the U.S. government to Indian Territory (now Oklahoma). They took many of their traditions with them, including their use of the devil's shoestring. This creative fishing method was documented on film during the 1920s by librarian and amateur naturalist Jennie Elrod. Her photographs provide a lasting visual document of one of the Creek Indians' traditions.

Creek fishermen spread the powdered devil's shoestring into a pool of still water.

A group of Creek men and boys wade around in the water to evenly distribute and mix in the poison.

A Creek man begins to gather the stunned fish by shooting them with a bow and arrow.

A 1905 map of the proposed Indian state, Sequoyah. Indian Territory tribal leaders suggested to the U.S. government the creation of Sequoyah as an alternative to the incorporation of Indian Territory into the new state of Oklahoma.

(continued from page 107)

up their towns. Their farms were fertile and productive, and many families raised crops adequate to their needs. Provisions written into the allotment legislation prohibited Creek owners from selling their property, and thus they were protected for a while from the swindles and sharp deals of real estate speculators. By the 1920s much of this had changed. When original allottees died and their children inherited their farms, problems arose over how the land should be divided. A farm that would support one family could not support several. But as long as the sale of land was restricted, a Creek heir could not purchase the land of his or her siblings in order to consolidate the farm. The restrictions caused hardships, and many Creeks began to demand that they be lifted. If the Creeks were to be full-fledged citizens of the United States, they argued, they should have the same rights to own, sell, or buy land as did other Americans.

The government gradually lifted the restrictions, allowing Creeks to buy and sell their land. But without the protection offered by the restrictions, many Creeks became victims of their own unfamiliarity with the concepts of private ownership and of unscrupulous whites who took advantage of that lack of familiarity. Some Creeks lost their land because the U.S. government made void a law barring taxation of the Indians' allotments. They did not understand the idea of property taxes and lost their farms to cover those expenses. Others mortgaged their farms to buy goods, only to lose their land through foreclosure when they could not pay their debts.

Real estate speculators, of course, were among the greatest supporters of lifting the restrictions. They hoped to take advantage of the unsophisticated Indians and buy their allotments cheaply. Furthermore, swindlers of all kinds descended upon the Indians of the Five Tribes. With their political power in the new state and better knowledge of laws, they succeeded in cheating thousands of Creeks out of their property. Some moved from unethical to outright criminal acts. One of the most scandalous tactics involved promising elderly Indians monthly payments of $10 for life in exchange for the title to their allotment. Many people signed and then died mysteriously within weeks.

The Dawes Commission had originally recommended that the tribes, rather than individuals, retain ownership of valuable minerals. The Creeks argued that if their nation was to be allotted, then their land's resources, including minerals, should be privately owned. The commissioners deferred, and the Creeks' allotment agreement made official the Indians' position on this issue. Then oil was discovered.

Tulsa, an old Creek town on the Arkansas River, was at the southern end of a huge underground lake of oil. But in 1901, when it was discovered, allotment had not been completed. The Creeks' allotment agreement did not allow them to lease their lands to oil companies for resource development. Eager to tap this unexpected wealth, representatives from the Creek Nation and the United States drafted a supplement to the allotment agreement that outlined a leasing program.

Soon after the Creeks settled the leasing agreement, the Glenn Oil Pool was discovered. This phenomenally rich source was first encountered just south of Tulsa on the allotment of the Glenn family. They and other Creek owners of allotments in that part of the Nation quickly found themselves fabulously rich as they began to collect the several thousand dollars a month paid to them by oil companies. Such wealth naturally attracted hordes of dishonest people who went to great lengths to rob the Creeks of their oil rights and revenues.

As members of a culture that traditionally held land in common, many Creeks had little experience in managing private land. Few had a working knowledge of the use of money, either. Therefore, when they found themselves thrust into the world of white American economic values, the Creeks were unable to anticipate possible dangers or problems. There was no way for them to protect their interests and property from the land-hungry real estate brokers, tax courts, and oil company lawyers. Allotment, designed to break up tribal governments and communities and encourage Indian people to enter the mainstream of American society, succeeded mainly in robbing Creeks and other Indians of their property and reducing them to a state of utter poverty.

To help the Creeks manage their property, the Oklahoma state government developed a system by which the county courts appointed guardians for some Creeks. These guardians took over the management of allotments belonging to those Indians who could not speak English, adults as well as children. Often the Indians never again saw their land, the proceeds from its sale, or the revenues from oil leases. Among the most vulnerable were Creek children, particularly orphans. In 1909, Oklahoma Commissioner of Charities and Corrections

Kate Barnard found three small children living in a hollow tree, scavenging for food. Their parents were dead, and it took Barnard six weeks to locate their court-apppointed guardian. She then discovered that the children owned Glenn Pool allotments but that their guardian had lied to the court about money he claimed to have spent on their education and support. He had been living off their oil royalties as well as those of 51 other children for whom he was responsible.

By the end of the 1920s, the allotment policy began to come under criticism. Antiallotment reformers and others, such as Barnard, cited the growing poverty and

Children of the Glenn family, photographed in about 1906. These youths were heirs to a fortune after oil was discovered on their parents' allotment.

homelessness of Indians, the failure to integrate them into mainstream American society, and the increasing evidence of fraud and corruption in the administration of the allotment process as more than enough reason to revoke it. These critics aroused the interest of several congressmen, whose investigations convinced them that changes had to be made. The stock market crash of 1929 and the subsequent Great Depression increased the general feeling in the United States that the government ought to help the Indians.

When Franklin D. Roosevelt was elected president in 1932, most government officials favored a strong change in federal Indian policy. In response, Roosevelt appointed a reformer, Harold Ickes, as secretary of the interior, and Ickes, in turn, appointed John Collier as commissioner of Indian affairs. Both men believed in reversing allotment policy, and in 1934 they convinced Congress to enact the Indian Reorganization Act (IRA). The act not only halted allotment; it authorized the return to tribal communities, the reorganization of tribal governments with constitutions, the purchase of land to be owned in common by tribal members, the establishment of tribal corporations for economic development and of several loan funds to underwrite individual and tribal needs.

Although the IRA seemed to be the answer to the Indians' dilemma, senators, congressmen, and many of the Indian leaders from Oklahoma opposed it. They claimed that in Oklahoma allotment

In 1909, Commissioner Kate Barnard uncovered abuses in the U.S. government's system of providing guardians for Creek orphans. The people appointed to care for Creek children and their allotments often took their wards' money and property and left the youngsters to starve.

had progressed too far, it was too late to recreate tribalism, and in any case it was wrong to try. Their arguments were effective, and the federal government exempted tribes in Oklahoma from the IRA. Commissioner Collier and Oklahoma senator Elmer Thomas then traveled through the state consulting with the Indians for legislation that would fit their special needs. When the two men were done, Thomas wrote the bill that passed Congress as the Oklahoma Indian Welfare Act (OIWA) in 1936. It contained the same provisions as the IRA for tribal incorporation and federal loans and authorized the purchase of lands to be held in trust by the secretary of the interior for the use of tribal groups, and unlike the IRA, it also provided for constitutional, rather than tribal, governments. Although it was too late to reverse all the damage done by allotment, the OIWA nevertheless contained the seeds of positive change for the Creeks and the other Indians of Oklahoma.

The Creeks had weathered the bad effects of allotment better than any other Oklahoma tribe. They had more fertile farmland, and many families had been able to hang on to their allotments despite the efforts of swindlers to take them. In addition, events had not seriously disrupted their settlement patterns. This meant that the ancient system of social and political organization by towns had more or less survived intact. In some ways, the towns had thrived. Allotment had released the traditional Creeks from the interference of the constitutional government leaders. It returned to the towns the main responsibilities for government. The towns had few legal resources and were not always able to help their people against the political power of the whites. They were, however, an enormously important source of social and cultural support for the Creek people. Through the operation of traditional town and clan obligations, the people were able to over-

come the worst effects of their poverty. Thus, when the OIWA went into effect in the late 1930s, the Creeks were able to take advantage of its opportunities.

Despite the Curtis Act, allotment, and statehood, the leadership of the Creek Nation also had never absolutely ceased to exist. The National Council and the courts closed down, but the positions of principal and town chiefs continued, providing an important semblance of leadership for the Creeks. These chiefs were appointed by the president and had no official power, but they spoke for the combined interests of the people and performed an important function simply by their visibility. The OIWA, with its provisions for establishing tribal corporations and regaining tribal lands, provided the Creeks with the means to recreate some of their national institutions. As in the old days, the Council represented the towns, thus keeping alive the tradition of town influence in national political affairs.

In some ways, however, town interests continued to dominate Creek affairs, preventing the Indians from creating a national political agenda. For example, during the 1940s and 1950s, towns lost many of their inhabitants to the armed forces in World War II. The population decline continued after the war when large numbers of Creeks, many of whom had become acquainted with off-reservation life while in the service, left their home to find work in the cities. Therefore, it grew more difficult for the town councils to continue their political roles. But town leaders continued to concern themselves with local, rather than national, issues. Furthermore, the Creeks had no real sense of loyalty for the office of principal chief, either. As long as the principal chief was appointed by the president, the Creek people were reluctant to grant him much power. Thus, national political affairs became increasingly confused.

By the 1950s, however, the center of power had gradually shifted away from the towns to the national capital at Okmulgee. This tendency continued, so that when the popular election of the principal chief returned to the Creek people in 1971 under Congressional authorization, the new pattern of strong executive leadership was well established. Claude Cox was elected during that year and has held that office for nearly 20 years. During this time, he has presided over the continued revival of the Creek Nation. Such efforts at the national level included the construction of a Creek capital complex in Okmulgee to house tribal and BIA offices, the increase of federal health care services, the development of programs to provide better educational

Creek women preparing to perform a traditional stomp dance at the Creek tribal dance grounds in Eufaula, Oklahoma, in 1986. Around their legs they are wearing rattles made from turtle shells and tin cans.

The Creek Nation capital complex at Okmulgee, Oklahoma. The structure was designed to resemble a Mississippian mound.

and employment opportunities, and the construction of low-cost housing for low-income Creeks. The Nation has also implemented various agriculture-related businesses, including cattle raising, and opened a high stakes bingo parlor on tribal land in Tulsa.

In one of the most significant and controversial accomplishments of Cox's administration, the Creeks adopted a new constitution in 1975 to replace the old constitution of 1867. The new document provided for a strong executive office and a national council of representatives elected from eight geographic districts. This last provision has generated a familiar controversy because many Creeks still prefer council representation by town—the traditional political unit that dates back to their beginning and that sustained them during the allotment years.

Unlike the Indians in most states, the Creeks in Oklahoma do not live on a reservation. The only tribally owned lands they have are tracts for the capital complex, various businesses, and housing and health facilities. Most Creeks live on privately owned farms in the region of the old Creek Nation and in the towns and cities of eastern Oklahoma. For all practical purposes, they live much like their non-Indian neighbors. But their lives differ in several important ways. Because they are Creeks, they have a history that is unique to them, they have a tribal government, and for those who choose to participate, they have their summer ceremonies at their festival centers, known as stomp grounds.

The Creeks who remained in the east, known as the Poarch Creek Band, have also been rebuilding their heritage. During the early 20th century, the majority of the Poarch Creeks lost their land and became sharecroppers (people who farm someone else's land for a share in the produce) or day laborers in Alabama's timber industry. In 1939, the state provided them with an Indian elementary school, and in 1950 they were allowed to attend a nearby non-Indian public high school. The Poarch Creeks made further advances when they shared in the Oklahoma Creeks' 1962 victory in a court case against the federal government. This victory encouraged the Poarch Creeks to elect a council, organize an annual powwow, and seek recognition from the federal government as a tribe. In 1980, the United States conferred official tribal status on the Poarch Band and extended the services of the BIA, including health care and educational benefits, to them. The several hundred members of the eastern Creeks continue to maintain the presence of the once-powerful Creek Nation on its traditional homeland.

Although Creek towns no longer have official status in the national government, they continue to be important in the life of many Creeks. On specified days, mem-

Claude Cox, who was elected principal chief in 1971. During his administration, the Creek Nation began to revive its economy.

bers of a town still gather at its square ground to consume the ceremonial drink that brings physical and spiritual purification. They listen to the stories and advice of their elders, and they join in dances that have religious as well as social significance. Participation in town and ceremonial functions links modern Creeks to one another and to the distant past when the Creek people first climbed out of the earth's mouth and began their journey through space and time. ▲

BIBLIOGRAPHY

Debo, Angie. *And Still the Waters Run: The Betrayal of the Five Civilized Tribes*. Princeton: Princeton University Press, 1940.

———. *The Five Civilized Tribes of Oklahoma: Report on Social and Economic Conditions*. Philadelphia: Indian Rights Association, 1951.

———. *The Road to Disappearance*. Norman: University of Oklahoma Press, 1941.

Grayson, George Washington. *A Creek Warrior for the Confederacy*. Edited by W. David Baird. Norman: University of Oklahoma Press, 1988.

Green, Donald E. *The Creek People*. Phoenix: Indian Tribal Series, 1973.

Green, Michael D. *The Creeks: A Critical Bibliography*. Bloomington: Indiana University Press, 1979.

———. *The Politics of Indian Removal: Creek Government and Society in Crisis*. Lincoln: University of Nebraska Press, 1982.

Opler, Morris. "The Creek 'Town' and the Problem of Creek Indian Political Reorganization." In *Human Problems in Technological Change*, edited by Edward H. Spicer, 162–80. New York: Russell Sage Foundation, 1952.

Paredes, J. Anthony. "Back from Disappearance: The Alabama Creek Indian Community." In *Southeastern Indians Since the Removal Era*, edited by Walter L. Williams, 123–41. Athens: University of Georgia Press, 1979.

Swanton, John R. *Myths and Tales of the Southeastern Indians*. Washington, DC: U.S. Government Printing Office, 1929.

THE CREEKS AT A GLANCE

TRIBE   *Creek (Muskogee)*

CULTURE AREA   *Southeast*

GEOGRAPHY   *Georgia and Alabama until removal in 1835; eastern Oklahoma after removal*

LINGUISTIC FAMILY   *Muskogean*

CURRENT POPULATION   *Approximately 30,000*

FIRST CONTACT   *Hernando de Soto, Spanish, 1540*

FEDERAL STATUS   *Recognized*

GLOSSARY

agent A person appointed by the Bureau of Indian Affairs to supervise U.S. government programs on a reservation and/or in a specific region. After 1908 the title *superintendent* replaced *agent*. The British colonial government in the 1700s also referred to those who acted as liaisons with Indian groups as agents.

agriculture Intensive cultivation of tracts of land, sometimes using draft animals and heavy plowing equipment. Agriculture requires a heavily nonnomadic life.

allotment U.S. policy applied nationwide in 1887 through the General Allotment Act (also known as the Dawes Severalty Act or Dawes Act) aimed at breaking up tribally owned reservations by assigning individual farms and ranches to Indians. Allotment was intended as much to discourage traditional communal activities as to encourage private farming and the assimilation of Indians into mainstream American life.

annuity Compensation for land and/or resources based on terms of a treaty or other agreement between the United States and an individual tribe. Annuities consisted of goods, services, and cash given to the tribe every year for a specified period.

anthropology The study of the physical, social, and historical characteristics of human beings.

archaeologist A scientist who studies past human societies through the objects, records, and settlements that people leave behind.

archaeology The recovery and reconstruction of human ways of life through the study of material culture (including tools, clothing, food, and human remains).

band A loosely organized group of people who are bound together by the need for food and defense, by family ties, and/or by other common interests.

breechcloth A strip of animal skin or cloth that is drawn between the legs and hung from a belt tied around the waist.

Bureau of Indian Affairs (BIA) A U.S. government agency now within the Department of the Interior. Originally intended to manage trade and other relations with Indians, the BIA now seeks to develop and implement programs that encourage Indians to manage their own affairs and to improve their educational opportunities and general social and economic well-being.

chakofa A communal town house in which Creek leaders held their councils during the winter. The building was located next to the square ground in each Creek town and housed the town's ceremonial fire.

chiefdom A complex series of social and political organizations that had one ruler who held absolute authority over the people of a particular region.

clan A multigenerational group having a shared identity, organization, and property based on belief in descent from a common ancestor. Because clan members consider themselves closely related, marriage within most clans is strictly prohibited.

culture The learned behavior of humans; nonbiological, socially taught activities; the way of life of a group of people.

Curtis Act Passed by Congress in 1898, a bill that mandated allotment, abolished the tribal court system, and required that all laws passed by tribal governments be approved by the president of the United States.

Department of the Interior A U.S. government office created in 1849 to oversee the internal affairs of the United States, including government land sales, land-related legal disputes, and American Indian affairs.

Devil's Shoestring A poisonous herb that Creek men would pound into a powder and sprinkle into a still body of water. The mixture, poisonous to the pond's inhabitants, would stun fish, causing them to float to the surface where the fishermen could simply gather them up.

Indian Reorganization Act (IRA) The 1934 federal law, sometimes known as the Wheeler-Howard Act, that ended the policy of allotting plots of land to individual Indians and encouraged the development of reservation communities. The act also provided for the creation of autonomous tribal governments.

Indian Territory An area in the south-central United States to which the U.S. government resettled Indians from other regions, especially the eastern states. In 1907, the territory was incorporated into lands that became the state of Oklahoma.

Italwa In the Muskogee language, the Creek word for a village. After the arrival of the English, the italwas came to be commonly known as towns.

matrilineal kinship Rules for determining family or clan membership by tracing kinship through female ancestors. In this system children are considered to be related to their mother and all her clan kin but not to their father or his clan kin.

matrilocality The practice in which newly married Creek couples moved into the compound of the wife and her clan relatives.

mico The Muskogee word for *chief.*

mission A religious center founded by advocates of a particular denomination who are trying to convert nonbelievers to their faith.

Mississippian An Indian civilization so named because it began in the central Mississippi River valley of North America in approximately A.D. 600.

mound A large earthen construction built by pre-historic American Indians as a base for a public building or to contain human graves.

Muskogee A term by which many modern Creeks refer to themselves, it is also used to signify the language that most of them speak.

poskita A late summer celebration, known also as the Green Corn Ceremony, during which the Creeks gave thanks for the new corn crop, honored the renewal of life in the new year, and recounted the history and laws of the town. With dance and oratory, the Creeks ceremonially cleansed themselves of their misdeeds and forgave others their wrongs.

removal policy Federal policy, initiated in 1830, that called for the sale of all Indian land in the eastern and southern United States and the migration of the Indians from these areas to land west of the Mississippi River.

reservation, reserve A tract of land retained by Indians for their own occupation and use. *Reservation* is used to describe such land in the United States; *reserve* in Canada.

square ground The large, open, rectangular space that was traditionally the ceremonial and political center of every Creek town. During the summer months, the Creeks entertained visitors, held council meetings, and conducted religious ceremonies in their town squares.

termination Federal policy, in effect from the late 1940s through the 1960s, instituted to remove Indian tribes from government supervision and Indian lands from trust status.

territory A defined region of the United States that is not but may become a state. The government officials of a territory are appointed by the president, but territory residents elect their own legislature.

theocracy A form of government in which the political leaders and the religious leaders are the same people.

treaty A contract negotiated between representatives of the U.S. government or another national government and one or more Indian tribes. Treaties dealt with the cessation of military action, the establishment of land boundaries, terms of land sales, and related matters.

tribe A society consisting of several or many separate communities united by kinship, culture, language, and other social institutions including clans, religious organizations, and warrior societies.

trust The relationship between the federal government and many Indian tribes, dating from the late 19th century. Government agents managed Indians' business dealings, including land transactions and rights to national resources, because the Indians were considered legally incompetent to manage their own affairs.

weir A wooden fence or a rock wall constructed in a stream to trap fish or force them into a narrow channel where they can easily be netted.

INDEX

PICTURE CREDITS

Courtesy of the Alabama Department of Archives and History, pages 29, 34, 54;
W. Bartram, "American Ethnological Society, Transactions," 1853: in Peter Nabokov and
Robert Easton's *Native American Architecture*, copyright Nabokov and Easton, by permission
of Oxford University Press, Inc., page 22; Bettman, pages 19, 30, 39, 40; Culver Pictures
Inc., page 36; Courtesy of the Georgia Department of Archives and History, pages 44, 56,
62; Field Museum of Natural History, Neg. No. A93851, Chicago, page 47; Five Civilized
Tribes Museum, Muskogee, page 87 (photo by Jim Fowler); Gibbs Museum of Art/Carolina
Art Association, page 28; Thomas Gilcrease Institute of American History and Art, Tulsa,
Oklahoma, pages 45, 59, 112; Courtesy of Daryl Lamb/Butts County Historical Society,
page 61; Library of Congress, page 69 (LC US262-435); Muscogee (Creek) Nation
Communication Center, pages 21 (painting by Larry McMurtry), 115 (photo by Elliot
Barnett), 116 (photo by Gary Robinson), 117 (photo by Gary Robinson); Courtesy of the
Museum of the American Indian, Heye Foundation, pages 51, 98, 103, 104; Museum of the
City of Mobile, page 48; National Park Service/Ocmulgee National Monument, pages 15,
16; Courtesy of the New York Historical Society, New York City, page 81; North Carolina
Division of Archives and History, page 52; Archives and Manuscripts Division of the
Oklahoma Historical Society, pages 100, 107, 110, 113; From the collection of the State
Museum of History, Oklahoma Historical Society/photographed by Jim Smith, pages 73, 79
(top), 80 (bottom); Oklahoma Museum of Natural History, University of Oklahoma, pages 12
78 (top), 80 (top); Smithsonian Institution, National Anthropological Archives, pages 12
(negative # 1129-C), 24 (negative # 1169-B-1), 26 (pictograph 8), 43 (negative # 1169-A), 64
(negative # 45.111-F), 92 (negative # 1109), 97 (negative # 1108); Photographed by Michael
Latil, Department of Anthropology, Smithsonian Institution, cover (negative # 31549),
pages 75 (catalogue # 358206), 76 (catalogue # 272989), 77 (top; catalogue # 342066), 77
(bottom; catalogue # 315090), 78–79 (catalogue # 272988); Courtesy of the Tennessee State
Museum, Vanderbilt University Thruston Collection, page 18 (photo by June Dorman);
Tiger Art Gallery, page 70 (painted by the Late Jerome Tiger); Reproduced by the
permission of the Trustees of the British Museum, page 74; Western History Collection,
University of Oklahoma Library, pages 84, 88, 93, 95, 102.

Maps (pages 33, 67, 82, 91) by Gary Tong.

MICHAEL D. GREEN is associate professor of history and chair of Native American Studies at Dartmouth College. He holds a B.A. in history from Cornell College, an M.A. and Ph.D. in history from the University of Iowa, and was a postdoctoral fellow at the D'Arcy McNickle Center for the History of the American Indian at the Newberry Library. Professor Green is the author of *The Politics of Indian Removal: Creek Government and Society in Crisis* and *The Creeks: A Critical Bibliography*, as well as numerous articles and book chapters on Creek and Mesquakie history.

FRANK W. PORTER III, general editor of INDIANS OF NORTH AMERICA, is director of the Chelsea House Foundation for American Indian Studies. He holds a B.A., M.A., and Ph.D. from the University of Maryland. He has done extensive research concerning the Indians of Maryland and Delaware and is the author of numerous articles on their history, archaeology, geography, and ethnography. He was formerly director of the Maryland Commission on Indian Affairs and American Indian Research and Resource Institute, Gettysburg, Pennsylvania, and he has received grants from the Delaware Humanities Forum, the Maryland Committee for the Humanities, the Ford Foundation, and the National Endowment for the Humanities, among others. Dr. Porter is the author of *The Bureau of Indian Affairs* in the Chelsea House KNOW YOUR GOVERNMENT series.